T0418548

LEADING TOWARD
LIBERATION

LEADING TOWARD
LIBERATION

*How to Build Cultures of Thriving
in Higher Education*

ANNMARIE CAÑO

JOHNS HOPKINS UNIVERSITY PRESS
Baltimore

All rights reserved. Published 2025
Printed in the United States of America on acid-free paper
2 4 6 8 9 7 5 3 1

Johns Hopkins University Press
2715 North Charles Street
Baltimore, Maryland 21218
www.press.jhu.edu

Library of Congress Cataloging-in-Publication Data

Names: Caño, Annmarie, 1971– author.
Title: Leading toward liberation : how to build cultures of thriving
in higher education / Annmarie Caño.
Description: Baltimore : Johns Hopkins University Press, 2025. |
Includes bibliographical references and index.
Identifiers: LCCN 2024033473 | ISBN 9781421451336 (hardcover ;
acid-free paper) | ISBN 9781421451343 (ebook)
Subjects: LCSH: Educational change—United States. | Educational
leadership—United States. | Education, Higher—United
States—Administration. | Educational psychology—United States.
Classification: LCC LB2806.23 .C36 2025 | DDC 378.1/07—dc23/eng/20241211
LC record available at https://lccn.loc.gov/2024033473

A catalog record for this book is available from the British Library.

*Special discounts are available for bulk purchases of this book. For more information,
please contact Special Sales at specialsales@jh.edu.*

For Lee,
Who grounds me so I can envision otros mundos posibles

CONTENTS

LEADING TOWARD
LIBERATION

CHAPTER 1

Introduction

New to my institution, I was excited to support new colleagues
and advance the mission of our unit and the university. For a
time, I was able to do just that, cocreating a culture that freed
people up to do their best work in alignment with their own and
the institution's stated values. As time went on, I realized that
our efforts were not enough. I couldn't put my finger on the
problem until I participated in a high-level leadership search.
Most of the search committee members would not express their
opinions before first asking the search committee chair, who was
also the hiring manager, about what the leader thought. This
was surprising because we were told that we were appointed to
the committee so we could contribute our valued opinions. As I
was the only person of color on this search committee, it became increasingly uncomfortable for me to ask questions, seek
clarification, or pause the conversation so we could reflect on
our decision-making process. When we arrived at our initial
slate of finalists—all white men—I raised my hand yet again
to request further discussion about a slate that did not include

other candidates who were also qualified to lead. While I was dismayed by the proceedings, things were starting to make sense. The system was designed to prevent the change I and others were trying to advance. Soon after, I chose to leave my leadership position and devote myself to writing this book about another possible way: leading toward liberation.

If you are like me, you have witnessed talented and caring students, postdocs, faculty, and staff resign their positions or leave our institutions because of unhealthy work environments. Some even have left academia altogether because of the harm it does. I have also witnessed people make excuses for these departures, deflecting institutional and personal responsibility: "They were a superstar and were not going to stay long anyway," or "They want to be closer to family because of the pandemic." The individuals who left told different stories. They could point to specific interactions and events that caused harm and created oppressive environments. In some cases, leaving a role or an institution was the only option to preserve one's health and wellness.

To counteract this trend, let's liberate the academic workplace from trauma and oppression. A cynical reader might ask, "This sounds all well and good, but why try when academia, itself a large and complex system, is situated within a society that is not free from oppression?" It might seem like a tall order to ask anyone to put in this effort. But I have caught glimpses of liberation, and chances are you have too. For instance, during a Zoom call just a few months into the pandemic and my tenure as a dean, an early-career faculty member of the global majority asked me if I was "for real." All of us on the call shared a hearty laugh, and then we unpacked the question. They had not experienced leaders who invited questions and feedback with compassion and without judgment, connecting with their struggles and inviting their ideas to cocreate a new path forward. It was a liberating moment for all of us and a chance to create something new. Showing up for liberation not only sustains leaders but also invites others to the work of creating healthier environments in which faculty, staff, and students can thrive. In turn, they are better able to meet the needs of others.

Leading toward liberation promotes health and wholeness through the liberation of systems and structures within which people work. Liberatory leaders, whether they have a formal title or not, engage in critical self-awareness rooted in historical and contemporary reality. They accompany others in solidarity and engage in courageous action to cocreate new ways of doing business that allow everyone, not just a privileged few, to flourish. A liberation mindset requires leaders at every level to continually grow into a reflective practice to resist and reject the oppression from which they may benefit.

This book serves as a call to action and a guide for emerging and seasoned leaders who want to be part of a liberating culture shift. By liberating the way we lead, we can collectively remake higher education into an engine of liberation for society at large. Leading with a liberation mindset is not easy because it pushes against the status quo. But together, we have the potential to cocreate academic cultures in which everyone can thrive.

My Liberation Journey

Through my own professional and personal journey, I have come to realize that surviving and thriving in academia requires a liberation mindset. Yet I lived much of my professional life without awareness that liberation was key. In fact, I thought education was the path to personal freedom in the form of financial independence and security. My immigrant father from Spain and my Puerto Rican mother instilled in me the meritocratic belief that is core to the American Dream: anything is possible if you work hard enough. I was not yet aware of how this "dream" was built on the genocide and theft of Indigenous people (Tallbear, 2019), nor was I aware of how this dream was racialized or infused with a colonial mentality (Comas-Díaz, 2022). Cracks began to appear when I hit college. I was a high school valedictorian, but as a first-generation college student, I was not prepared for academic challenges and unwritten Ivy League social norms. I struggled for two years, believing that perhaps they had made a mistake in admitting me; I internalized the norms of who belonged. Eventually, I stumbled onto great mentors and I learned how to "do college." I hit my stride in graduate school but experienced other barriers along my professional journey. For instance, as a faculty member, I often interpreted sexist, racist, and classist remarks as individual or one-off events. My psychology training focused on intrapersonal explanations of people's behavior and did not prepare me to recognize how systems of oppression were enacted through exclusionary, gatekeeping, and toxic behaviors, culture, and policy. It took some time to learn that no matter how much I worked, there might be policies, practices, or unspoken norms that would hold me back. In fact, it wasn't until my first leadership position outside my department that I began to understand the system for what it is: a system that oppresses and demands conformity to a narrow definition of success. I distinctly remember disclosing to a trusted senior colleague, a Black male scientist, that I felt embarrassed and guilty for not being aware of the effects of racism and sexism more plainly until then. I had lived in my marginalizations as a Latina and first-generation college student and had not recognized my own privilege as a light-skinned, white-appearing person. He listened and then encouraged me by responding that I was now in a position to contribute to systemic change. Additional experiences, intentional learning, and aha moments over time led me to adopt an approach that is liberatory, not only for myself but for others.

Why Liberation Matters in Higher Education

Core to a liberation mindset is reading contemporary and historical reality. To understand why liberation matters, we must examine the current state of higher education and how we got here.

Contemporary Reality

Oppression shows up in the contemporary structures, policies, and norms that operate in higher education settings today. Most universities have a hierarchical structure with a strong president whose primary concerns are finances, operations, and reputation. Presidents are often referred to as the CEOs of the institution. With the decline in public funding and shifting expectations of a higher education, colleges and universities have become increasingly corporatized, with a focus on revenue generation, entrepreneurship, and money-saving tactics including an increased reliance on adjunct and contract labor (Cottom, Hunnicutt, and Johnson, 2018). Enrollment declines that began even before the pandemic (Irwin et al., 2023) have tightened the focus on revenues and savings. Presidents and their cabinets are also challenged with managing deferred maintenance on physical structures, personnel expenditures due to rising inflation, insurance, the mishandled rollout of the revised Free Application for Federal Student AID (FAFSA), and other costs while also facing dwindling funding from states and increased competition for students and benefaction. In the past decade, many colleges and universities have closed because of financial exigency and insolvency (Barshay, 2022; Castillo and Welding, 2023; Higher Ed Dive, 2023). These dynamics have contributed to increased competition among colleges and universities for tuition-paying students. The push to generate revenue creates tensions for faculty, staff, and students down the line.

Against the backdrop of these financial stressors, the value of a college education is being challenged. Surveys show that most Americans (56 percent) believe that college is not worth the expense (Lederman, 2023). Administrators turn to program prioritization and market analyses to decide which programs to grow and which to close, affecting the livelihoods of faculty and staff as well as the creation of knowledge. Writing before the pandemic, Amit Mrig and Patrick Sanaghan (2017) stated that many of these higher education leadership challenges are adaptive in nature; they are challenges for which we do not have a blueprint or map. Yet leaders have not shifted *how* they lead to deal with these challenges. Often, the way they make decisions results in oppression and toxicity. Leadership books and programs continue to focus on business acumen, conflict management, and other traditional leadership skills. To lead differently, however, leaders must acknowledge the ways our contemporary realities are rooted in oppressive histories.

Historical Reality

A closer look at the history of higher education in the United States suggests we should not be surprised with our current state. While we often tout the ideals of higher education, including progress, social mobility, and the public good, these ideals are also a product of settler colonialism, including the forcible taking of land from Indigenous peoples and nations and the exclusion of people from higher education such as enslaved Africans, indentured servants, and immigrants (Stein, 2022). Thus, universities in the United States are rooted in and continue to reap the benefits of settler colonialism and genocide. For instance, the founding of most higher education institutions in the United States was made possible by the concept of the settler nation-state and the Doctrine of Discovery of the fifteenth century. This doctrine endorsed Christian European conquest and colonization of non-Christian people around the globe. It was then adopted by the US Supreme Court as law in the early 1800s to give land to European "discoverers" (Dunbar-Ortiz, 2015). One example is the Morrill Act of 1862, which permitted states to create public universities on land stolen from Indigenous tribes and communities. White Europeans killed and ejected Indigenous people from their lands, which set the stage for universities to take control of the lands and replace ways of teaching, learning, and knowing.

In the United States, settler colonialism and enslavement are intertwined with our capitalist roots. Universities in the United States were made possible by market forces that privileged wealthy, white Protestant men (Labaree, 2017). The first universities were private and tuition driven. Even though public institutions were later established, including through the Morrill

Acts, state support has declined since peaking in the mid-twentieth century. Competitive capitalistic revenue generation continues to be key to success for American colleges and universities. David F. Labaree also explains that capitalistic influences are not restricted to budgeting; these influences filter into the institutional culture. For instance, the primacy of the research university has led to the worship of individual scholars, the commodification of their products, and competition for individual recognition and support. Likewise, universities in the United States continue to reproduce dispossession and enslavement by controlling the types and methods of knowledge that are permitted to be produced and taught (González Stokas, 2023).

Repeating History

The global coronavirus pandemic has revealed the impact of higher education's oppressive history in new ways. Institutions are beginning to take note of the increasing number of students with food and housing insecurity (Weissman, 2022) and mental health challenges (Flannery, 2023), in addition to similar difficulties facing university employees (American Association of Colleges and Universities, 2020; Bourgeault, Mantler, and Power, 2021). Faculty and staff have also begun to recognize that gatekeeping and exclusion, overwork, and toxic interpersonal interactions are taking a toll on their quality of life and work (Pope-Ruark, 2022). The 2020 police murders of George Floyd, Breonna Taylor, and other Black people also contributed to an awakening among many academics, some of whom recognized for the first time that inequities and injustices in society were also operating in our colleges and universities.

Many leaders turned to diversity, equity, and inclusion (DEI) initiatives to address injustice and inequity in order to counter institutional oppression. Unfortunately, some of these initiatives have been counterproductive. Ariana González Stokas (2023) notes that diversity, social justice, and antiracism work ends up accumulating Black, Indigenous, and other bodies so that universities can profit through greater prestige and dollars. This work may redistribute some power and privilege, but it also continues to uphold the power and privilege of oppressive leaders to function. In addition, oppressive forces outside the university are undermining DEI efforts. A growing movement of political actors claims that DEI is divisive, discriminatory, and a form of indoctrination. In some US states, fundamental knowledge about the human experience (e.g., with a focus on sex, gender, or race) has been deemed dangerous or false, leading to teaching and book bans and the elimination of curricula. Likewise, programs and offices aimed at creating a culture of affirmation and belonging for students who have experienced persistent marginalization and discrimination have been defunded and closed at many universities (see Gretzinger et al., 2024, which tracks these changes by US state). These attempts send a clear signal of who is (un)welcome and who continues to have power.

The Opportunity

Even before the pandemic, status quo leadership prioritized power, finances, and prestige over the dignity of people. As I talk to colleagues at different kinds of institutions, I hear time and again about the result: a stressed-out and demoralized workforce and high turnover or intentions to leave. In turn, students are not receiving the attention and high-quality education they deserve. Together, we have an opportunity to identify solutions to free us from this harmful spiral. González Stokas (2023, 46) offers that "the work of reparation is an undoing of present systems that enact oppression and violence" by centering those who have been oppressed in the decision-making process to advance systemic change. The leaders we need now are people who choose a path that creatively liberates the system so that everyone is free enough to contribute their talents, knowledge, and skills for the common good. The leaders we need now are those who choose liberation over oppression.

This book focuses on leaders at all levels because they are in a position to use their power and authority in service of liberating the environment. Leaders, whether titled or not, serve as *animadores* (animators or facilitators) who model culture through their public communications, relationships, priorities, and decisions. I have witnessed the clearest examples of liberatory leadership by people with the least amount of power. They did not have a title or formal authority, but they did have a strength of conviction, the courage to take risks, and the imagination to envision a different reality in which they and others can be more free. To be sure, higher education needs leaders who know how to balance a budget and engage in other responsible leadership tasks. But these leaders must also recognize and counteract oppression in all its forms. This book offers leaders a guide to practicing liberatory leadership skills.

What Is Leadership for Liberation?

Leadership for liberation is a way of influencing that promotes health and wholeness through the liberation of systems and structures in the workplace. To lead with liberation in mind, emerging and seasoned leaders develop and follow a personal mission that is grounded in the reality of the context in which they find themselves. This means we must have a realistic understanding of the forces at play, including white supremacy, heteropatriarchy, and ongoing colonization, all of which are reproduced in our higher education environments.

Liberatory leadership is grounded in the hope-filled belief that we have the capacity to participate in systemic healing of the wounded world in which we live. It means that we use our imagination to collectively cocreate with others the conditions to free ourselves from systems and ideologies that limit us and cause harm. It grounds individual experiences and choices within larger systems. Sexual harassment, workplace bullying, burnout from diversity and inclusion work, exhaustion from pandemic-related impacts on caregiving and scholarship, not to mention inadequate or harmful responses from institutions and leaders when people speak up about the harm done to them—all of these stressors and traumas are grounded in the cultures in which we work. If we try to address each event as its own isolated challenge, we can become mired in fixing individual problems, which can be exhausting and demoralizing. Instead, we need to situate individual problems within systems of oppression. Leadership for liberation identifies and exposes those systems while centering those who have been marginalized and oppressed, including but not limited to Black, Indigenous, and people of color (BIPOC) across genders, women across races, LGBTQ+ people, people with disabilities, and untenured faculty and staff. This kind of leadership also recognizes that the most marginalized are people from communities that have been harmed by multiple intersecting systems of oppression (Crenshaw, 1989).

Leadership for liberation is expansive enough to include freedom from oppressive systems for those with power and privilege. The liberatory leader recognizes that everyone is harmed by oppression. Critical educator Paulo Freire ([1970] 2000, 56) writes, "As the oppressors dehumanize others and violate their rights, they themselves also become dehumanized." This is a key facet of leadership for liberation, which recognizes that those with power and privilege have also been harmed by unrealistic and narrow expectations. In fact, most of us hold a collection of identities, some of which are privileged and others of which are oppressed and disempowered. So a leadership for liberation is a leadership for all. When we transform our institutional cultures with a liberatory mindset, we can work more creatively with our communities to effectively address problems that affect everyone, including climate change, income inequality, housing and food insecurity, and more.

Origins of Leadership for Liberation

This book is grounded in the psychology of liberation, a field founded by Ignacio Martín-Baró, who was a Spanish Jesuit priest, psychologist, and professor at the Universidad Centroamericana (UCA) in El Salvador until his murder in 1989. He believed that the "concern of the social scientist should not be so much to explain the world as to transform it" (Martín-Baró, 1994, 19). To that end, the psychology of liberation is an approach to understanding and challenging oppression in the context of groups and systems. Martín-Baró advocated for a psychology that counters marginalization and seeks justice through critical reflection; the recognition of the impact of historical and present-day harms such as war, violence, and poverty;

and the need for systemic change to liberate individuals and communities. Martín-Baró applied liberation psychology to reveal and resist political and economic repression and violence in El Salvador in the 1970s and 1980s. For instance, he created the Institute of Public Opinion at the UCA, which conducted and published opinion surveys to document the lived experiences of the people of El Salvador. With data from the people, Martín-Baró and his collaborators countered the lies told by corrupt politicians and their allied media outlets.

Liberation psychology borrowed key precepts from liberation theology and philosophy, a field to which Martín-Baró's colleague, theologian and priest Ignacio Ellacuría, contributed. Liberation theology is a theology of salvation (Gutiérrez, 1988), a theology in which acts that bring about human freedom are required of believers in God. With Ellacuría at the helm as university rector (president) and Martín-Baró as provost, the Jesuit-run UCA was put in service of the people and became a center of scholarship and advocacy working with and for the most marginalized community members. The UCA Jesuits critiqued higher education as an oppressive system that cared more about elitism and credential building than the common good or the welfare of oppressed community members. Ellacuría proposed that "the university must embody and implement its professed dedication to changing social structures in its threefold functions of teaching, research, and social outreach" (1990, 200).

For their liberatory work in these domains and their outspoken commentary against oppressive forces in their country, Martín-Baró, Ellacuría, and four of their Jesuit colleagues (most of them professors), along with their housekeeper and her daughter, were assassinated at the university by US-trained Salvadoran government forces on November 16, 1989. It may be difficult to imagine presidents, provosts, and faculty willing to risk death for their community and for the truth. Liberatory leadership is inherently risky because it challenges the status quo. This may be why academia has many examples of leaders who appear to succumb easily to political pressure, forfeiting their integrity and freedom in the process. As political dynamics change in the United States, the UCA martyrs' model of leadership is particularly compelling. In fact, the liberatory leadership of the Jesuits at the UCA is all the more inspiring in light of the sociopolitical dynamics of their time.

Central American Sociopolitical Context

This book draws primarily from Latin American liberation thought, especially in the Salvadoran context. As described throughout this book, an accurate reading of historical and contemporary reality is key to liberation praxis (i.e., the practice of liberation). Therefore, it is helpful to contextualize the rise of Latin American liberation theory and practice to understand just how powerful this movement has been.

In the mid- to late twentieth century, El Salvador and other countries were key to a post–Cold War US foreign policy aimed at developing Central and South American countries into capitalist economies in order to neutralize the spread of communism in the Western Hemisphere. Rich landowners in Central American countries like El Salvador capitalized on this policy by collaborating with military and political officials to oppress and silence poor *campesinos* (peasants or farmers) and Indigenous peoples who attempted to organize and demand rights to education, work, and land. The US government backed efforts to fight Marxism by advising the Salvadoran government and training the military, which used propaganda and violence to repress, torture, and kill adults and children. The Catholic Church at the time exerted a great deal of cultural power and authority. Local Catholic officials and leaders were often aligned with military and wealthy landowners despite Catholic social teaching emphasizing the dignity of work and the importance of human rights. For instance, Catholic leaders encouraged priests, missionaries, and lay catechists to preach about personal holiness and salvation in the afterlife. They discouraged the people from engaging in collective action in the here and now.

At the same time, as a result of the Second Vatican Council (1962–1965), Catholics around the globe were reexamining what it meant to be actively engaged with and in the world. In 1968, the Catholic bishops of Latin America came together in Medellín, Colombia, to discuss the church's responsibility as their communities experienced increasing violence and repression at the hands of the military and government. At this meeting, the bishops affirmed a commitment known as the "preferential option for the poor." At their regional conferences and retreats in 1968 and 1969, the Jesuits also reaffirmed and articulated their commitment to a faith that does justice, including the preferential option for the poor. (For an extensive treatment of the sociopolitical and religious events of the time, see Lassalle-Klein, 2014.)

The preferential option requires that we take the side of those living in poverty. As liberation theologian Gustavo Gutiérrez (1988, xxvii) explains,

The ultimate reason for commitment to the poor and oppressed is not to be found in the social analysis we use, or in human compassion, or in any direct experience we ourselves may have of poverty. These are all doubtless valid motives that play an important part in our commitment. As Christians, however, our commitment is grounded, in the final analysis, in the God of our faith. . . . In other words, the poor deserve preference not because they are morally or religiously better than others, but because God is God, in whose eyes "the last are first."

By default, "neutrality," or refraining from taking sides in political debates, results in siding with powerful oppressors. Put another way, "thoughts and prayers" for people living in conditions of poverty are not sufficient; we side with oppressors when we refrain from undoing the conditions that created and maintain poverty. The preferential option centers the claims of marginalized people and compels us to listen to and work with them to create a more just world. Consistent with liberation approaches, the preferential option is directed toward the fullness of human freedom.

One outcome of this commitment to freedom was increasing support for the development of Comunidades Eclesiales de Base (CEBs; Christian Base Communities or Basic Christian Communities). As communities of laypeople, the CEBs engaged in liberating praxis (practice) that embraced their lived experiences and challenged the hierarchical and oppressive status quo in the Catholic Church and in society at large (see Gandolfo and Potter, 2022, for an excellent in-depth description and decolonial analysis of the CEBs in El Salvador). Some of their first actions were to teach people to read so they could begin to interpret their contemporary reality in light of oppression and liberation in the Bible. With the help of literate laypeople, priests, and religious sisters, people began to develop a critical awareness of the injustice they experienced. With a renewed sense of dignity and purpose, they began to organize and bring about just change for themselves and others. Perhaps unsurprisingly, the people's efforts to mobilize were met with repression from the government and the military: threats, disappearances, torture, assassinations, and massacres of entire communities. Priests and others who supported the CEBs were pressured to stop by Catholic authorities. In some cases, they were killed by military, paramilitary, or police agents—for example, Rutilio Grande, a Jesuit priest, was murdered in 1977 along with two companions on his way to pray a novena in his hometown.

Grande was a promoter of CEBs and helped train leaders and catechists. He was also a good friend of the recently appointed archbishop of San Salvador, Óscar Arnulfo Romero. The two clerics often argued about the role of priests in politics, with Romero questioning whether priests should take sides in what he saw as political debates. Over time and especially after the death of his friend Grande, the archbishop came to understand that he was called to work against systemic oppression more actively. He found support among the UCA Jesuits who were oriented toward liberating the university in order to liberate society. Using his status and his access to a radio station, Romero publicly and courageously named oppressive and violent actions, held people and institutions accountable, and called for change. For this work, a death squad assassinated Romero during a Mass with parishioners in March 1980. The civil war lasted approximately 12 years in El Salvador (1979–1992). More than 75,000 Salvadorans lost their lives during this time. Many are still unaccounted for.

The UCA Jesuits, Romero, Grande, CEB leaders, and many others knew they were risking their lives by working in the liberation space. They were compelled to act to advance a collective vision of human freedom that does not permit oppression in any sphere. Today, nearly 30 years later, the CEBs continue to celebrate and remember these leaders. On a recent trip to El Salvador, I had the opportunity to spend some time with members of the CEBs and those who knew the UCA Jesuits. I was struck by how they described these leaders even today. The UCA Jesuits and other leaders were open to being transformed by their relationships with the most marginalized and oppressed of society. They did not center their own positional power or their advanced degrees. They truly listened, with empathy and solidarity. They validated the reality in which people were living and affirmed their creativity to solve systemic problems. They used their power and privilege to advocate for systemic change to benefit everyone. Imagine how universities would operate if we practiced a leadership of liberation. As pressures mount for college and university leaders in the United States to embrace narrow definitions of freedom—not just academic freedom and free speech but also what truth is and who is allowed to know the truth—the Salvadoran example is timely and thought provoking.

Contemporary Psychologies of Liberation

Since its inception, liberation psychology has been enriched by scholars using multicultural, feminist, and racial justice approaches (see Comas-Díaz and Torres Rivera, 2020b, for an overview; Montero, 2016). In fact, Comas-Díaz and Torres Rivera (2020a) point out that there is no one liberation psychology; rather, there are liberation psychologies that continue to develop as realities change. For example, scholars are weaving together Black feminist liberation (womanist) and Latinx feminist *mujerista* approaches to develop a transnational feminist perspective (*womanista*) framework (Bryant-Davis and Comas-Díaz, 2016; Chavez-Dueñas and Adames, 2020).

For this book, I draw on these liberation psychologies, especially those rooted in Latin American liberation thought. I also cite works that embrace liberation and decolonial perspectives of education, culture, and spirituality. I also pull from scholarship on the ways that oppression and liberation show up in university and institutional contexts, including workplace bullying and institutional betrayal, white supremacy and racialization in organizations, and workplace exclusion and inclusion. By referring to thinkers across a variety of disciplines, I emphasize that the work of liberation is universally relevant. I also claim that liberation involves individual and systemic change. Leaders who are committed to liberation must work on themselves as they also collaborate with others to cocreate a system in which everyone can be free to thrive and flourish. It is a privilege to honor the legacies of Martín-Baró and other writers who have spent their lives sharing their wisdom, by writing what I hope is a useful book to support others in their pursuit of liberating change.

Basic Principles of Liberation Praxis

Readers who are familiar with trauma-informed approaches may wonder how liberatory leadership is different. Clinicians Nathan Gerbrandt, Randy Grieser, and Vicki Enns (2021, 6) explain that "trauma-informed workplaces understand the presence of trauma, acknowledge the role trauma can play in a person's life, and promote work environments that support individual and collective well-being of all staff and clients. They create a sense of belonging, connection, and safety through their attitudes, policies, and practices." Trauma-informed leaders presume that people may have experienced trauma outside the workplace and that care should be extended to them. Liberatory practice is consistent with this work, and it goes two steps further by acknowledging that (1) the workplace, including leaders, can cause the trauma, and (2) some people are more likely to experience trauma in the world and in academia because of systems of oppression. In addition, liberatory practice is about changing the system through individual and collective self-reflection and action (praxis).

Self-Reflection for Personal Liberation

Martín-Baró and other liberation practitioners have argued that psychologists must practice personal liberation to effectively resist and dismantle oppression in the world. Without working on ourselves, we cannot cocreate systems of freedom. We may instead come to believe that we are liberators or saviors when, in fact, this attitude is just another feature of oppressive leadership. Martín-Baró and others draw from Freire's ([1970] 2000) concept of *conscientizacao* (conscientization), in which one strives for critical consciousness and awareness of societal influences on one's stories, choices, and behaviors so that one can take informed action. Through conscientization, we become aware of the ways oppression has harmed us and resistance has healed us in the past and currently. This kind of critical reflection is absolutely necessary for those practicing liberatory leadership. Our individual actions can maintain systems of oppression or contribute to liberation. We are more ready to engage in the work of liberation when we understand how our choices are bigger than ourselves.

As an example, my choices and life experiences cannot be separated from my parents' experiences and the broader sociopolitical context of immigration and migration in the United States. My mother experienced poverty and early family separation in her native Puerto Rico before moving to New York with her uncle's family. Despite the lasting impacts of Spanish colonization and American imperialism, there were glimpses of resistance and liberation. For instance, my maternal *abuela* was a *curandera* (healer) in her village, and my mother became a healer and reconciler of relationships. My father's story includes his immigration from Spain because of poverty and the discrimination of linguistic minorities exacerbated by the rise of fascism during the Spanish Civil War. A teenager at the time, he did not want to leave, but his mother made the decision for them to join other family members who had immigrated previously. She found work running a boarding house in New York for other (mostly Spanish) immigrants and ensured her son found work too. Though they experienced difficulties, both of my parents had family that cared and advocated for them and cultural and linguistic safe havens in their new country. They also had access to decent jobs and places to live because they were racialized as white and chose a path of assimilation. For instance, they raised their children to speak English first because they believed this would make it easier for us to succeed, a decision my mother later regretted.

"My" choices to pursue a career as a clinical health psychologist, professor, and leader are a function of systems of oppression, including colonization, fascism, white supremacy, and the myth of the American Dream, as well as models of resistance and resilience to oppressions through healing and caring for others. All these facets are evident in my parents' lives and continue to create opportunities and tensions for my personal actions. For instance, if I focus on my individual choices without seeking to understand the context, I run the risk of reinforcing oppressive practices. I might miss the opportunity to examine how I benefit from oppressive systems in higher education that make it more difficult for others to succeed. I may also miss how these same systems permitted me to succeed under certain conditions. Instead, I may think that I am exceptional and pride myself on my hard work or innate talent. I may assume that others who do not succeed have not tried hard enough. I would not be seeking systemic change if I thought everything could be explained by individual effort. This is in fact how I viewed the world in my teens and 20s and is why I blamed myself for not initially succeeding in college. My ignorance of systemic oppression also contributed to confusion about why there were not more people like me in the professoriate, as well as a sense of helplessness. A leadership for liberation requires that we take an honest look at ourselves in sociopolitical contexts over time. We develop a "consciousness-in-action" that brings together reflective awareness with intentional action against racism and other systems of oppression (Quiñones-Rosado, 2020). Our choices cannot be separated from what is going on in the world, but we can show resilience and resistance by working together to create a world that is more free.

Liberation in Action

In addition to ongoing critical self-reflection, leadership for liberation demands action such as *acompañamiento* (accompaniment) with the people most affected by oppressive systems. This includes entering their reality by listening deeply, with empathy and without defensiveness. To do this effectively and consistently, leaders must accept that they will not often be the expert in the room. Leading with humility is a challenging task for those of us who were groomed to be leaders in patriarchal, top-down systems in which leaders are rewarded for directing the action of others and are believed to know all. But humility is necessary when walking with others. Without it, we undermine our own self-liberation and risk alienating the very people we are trying to accompany into a more hopeful future.

Leaders can also engage in acts of solidarity. Think of colleagues who included you in decision-making even if you didn't have the "right" title, advocated for and changed a process or policy to be more equitable, spoke up publicly about an injustice that affected you or your community, or stepped back for you to share your expertise and amplify your ideas (and gave you credit!). Leaders who engage in these actions offer an antidote to the harm and trauma caused by oppressive workplaces.

Finally, liberatory leadership requires collective action to put in place policies and procedures that overturn oppressive systems that limit the ability of people to be their best selves. It is not surprising that this type of leadership is often exemplified by people of the global majority and others who have experienced discrimination, harassment, and exclusion in the workplace. Those of us with marginalized identities, especially multiple marginalizations (e.g., due to racism and ableism), have directly experienced silencing, isolating, and undermining behaviors from colleagues and leaders. We've experienced the impact of oppressive policies and procedures, albeit differently depending on our individual identities and life experiences. These experiences may steel our resolve to create an alternative environment that supports health, wholeness, and community. Importantly, the aim is not to fix the people who are wounded but to fix the system to make it possible for others to be free and flourish. The aim is also not to create a false freedom that encourages people to do whatever they want, harming others in the process. The point is for us to create a freedom that enables us to choose the good for ourselves and others. To be sure, liberatory leadership may entail risks, especially for those with less job security and authority; however, collective action offers a way for leaders to share the risks, responsibilities, and rewards of this kind of leadership.

Outline of This Book

There are a number of guides that offer useful academic leadership advice, and I've found many of them helpful in my own journey. Yet I have not found a leadership guide that adequately addresses the interplay between critical self-reflection and practice, between individual work and systems work. I have not found a guide that goes beyond simply acknowledging that people may need to chart a different course. A liberatory leadership framework addresses this gap and accommodates the unique combination of marginalized and privileged identities we each have. Understanding how my marginalized identities (Latina, first-generation college student, hearing impaired, working-class origin, mother of a middle schooler) and privileged identities (white appearing, tenured professor, cisgender and straight, currently higher socioeconomic status) shape me and shape people's perceptions of me as a leader is necessary for me to practice liberatory leadership. In speaking with other people from identity groups that are not (yet) highly represented in academic leadership, I realize I am not alone in wanting something new.

In the pages that follow, I embrace a growth mindset (Dweck, 2006). As liberation psychologist Jesica Siham Fernández (2022, 107) points out, "One does not achieve or arrive at a point of liberation, but rather develops the critical consciousness and relational practices of solidarity to resist oppression and constantly strive for transformative justice in the company of others." Similarly, González Stokas (2023), applying the lenses of decolonization and reparation, writes that we should engage in ongoing peace-making actions, centering participation and leadership of those harmed, rather than a singular performative act. Each one of us is on a journey that we will not complete in this lifetime. This means that none of us can claim that we have arrived as liberatory leaders. Our actions will speak for themselves. Only the most vulnerable can assess whether we are living up to the practice. There will always be a tension for leaders with positional authority and power to practice leadership for liberation because we are in positions that are skewed toward reinforcing hierarchy and power differentials, especially in systems that have engaged in oppression. As Ada María Isasi-Díaz (1996) encourages us, we must refrain from being passive participants in oppressive structures. As you read, reflect, and act, check in with peers who will hold you accountable as you practice liberatory leadership.

This book offers a method to practice liberatory leadership. It does not map out how you should do this exactly because this depends on your own critical consciousness—who you are in this moment at this time in history—as well as your institutional, geographical, and cultural context. The goal is not to assimilate and re-create the violence, exclusion, or toxicity we have experienced but to cocreate a new vision and reality with others who share a liberating vision. As Gandolfo and Potter (2022, 7) observed of the CEBs, we need to practice an "epistemic delinking from coloniality" that creates space for multiple ways of knowing to envision *un otro mundo posible* (an other possible world).

Each chapter in this book applies liberation psychology and other bodies of evidence to illustrate how academic leaders can cocreate healthier cultures that counter oppressive systems in the academy. This guide for navigating and disrupting the status quo to promote freedom, healing, and growth for self and others addresses the following topics.

In chapter 2, Crafting a Liberatory Personal Mission, I explain that leaders must know themselves in context and, from that knowledge, articulate a values-based personal mission to guide them. Without a personal mission that embraces the practice of liberation for self and others, it is easy to get derailed or demoralized by the day-to-day challenges or overwhelming aspects that are a function of oppressive systems. I offer guidance to craft a values-based mission that includes critical self-awareness, *testimonio*, and accountability.

Leaders who are working toward liberation in their organizations know how to assess the system in which they are working. Chapter 3, Reading Reality to Support Liberating Actions, includes guidance for reading the historical and contemporary reality of our institutions to identify supports and obstacles to change. Assessing how oppression and liberation are codified in institutional documents, policies, procedures, and culture is key to strategizing liberating change across institutional types.

Because of the hierarchical nature of higher education, it is a challenge to both hold a leadership position and not reinforce oppressive practices and policies. In chapter 4, Accompanying

Others as a Liberatory Practice, I share how entering into the struggle with others and accompanying them is a necessary practice for leaders who want to cocreate healthier environments. Leaders must show vulnerability, listen empathically and nondefensively, and center and validate others' experiences to rectify systemic harms.

Courage is another characteristic of liberatory leadership. In chapter 5, Leading Courageously When It Matters Most, I offer examples of courageous actions that can empower others to engage in the collective work of liberation. Recognizing that this can be an especially challenging situation for leaders of color, I also offer strategies for dealing with the resistance or pushback when people with marginalized identities engage in bold action.

In addition to modeling courageous and liberatory leadership, academic leaders can contribute to institutional liberation by creating opportunities for leadership development in others. In chapter 6, Growing Liberatory Leadership Skills in Others, I provide a rationale for why developing others is essential for the leader engaged in liberation, for the institution, and for higher education in general. I also provide concrete ideas for removing obstacles and creating opportunities to develop the next generation of leaders at all levels who work for freedom.

Leadership that pushes against oppression can be draining work if we do not take care of ourselves. We will be misunderstood and criticized by some. Others will demand more of our time, lives, and emotional energy than we can give because they are thirsty for change. I address these realities in chapter 7, Safeguarding Your Peace. I offer suggestions for assessing what depletes and energizes leaders, as well as some solutions to protect one's peace so leaders have the energy to persist in the work of freeing up the culture so everyone can thrive.

Chapter 8, Assessing Your Next Steps in Leadership, recognizes that growth is a natural outcome of a leadership practice that emphasizes freedom. Leaders may discover through their work that they have outgrown their role or organization, that it is time for others to lead, or that a workplace is so depleting that it is damaging their own health. In this chapter, I offer self-reflection prompts to ascertain when and how to move on or let go.

Chapter 9, Parting Thoughts, offers hope for how liberatory leadership can transform higher education and provides some additional resources for continued reflection and action.

A Word About Words and Storytelling

I intentionally chose to write about liberatory leadership or leaders (rather than liberating leadership or liberating leaders) to prevent readers from falling into the trap of saviorism. Leaders who practice liberation are not out for personal glory or pats on the back for our good work. By using phrases like "practicing liberation" and "working toward liberation," I hope to convey that we are trying our best and we may make mistakes. All of us continue to grow into a liberatory practice.

Though I focus on leaders throughout the book, I use the word *leader* inclusively. This term includes people with formal leadership titles like *provost*, *dean*, *department chair*, and *director*, as well as those without formal titles who are already leading or aspiring to lead change efforts in their spheres of influence, including committees, offices and other workspaces, classrooms, and communities. The other reason I use the term *leader* is for everyone to embrace their call to leadership, which follows the work of the CEBs. In liberation praxis, a true leader is anyone who seeks freedom for themselves and facilitates freedom for and with others. Titles may indicate decision-making authority in an organizational chart, but they do not guarantee that the individual practices or models liberatory leadership.

I use the terms *BIPOC, people of color,* and *people of the global majority* because I want to respect the ways in which people may describe themselves while also honoring that language continues to adapt and change as the work of liberation moves forward. For instance, *global majority* signifies that while people of color may be marginalized and minoritized in the United States, there is strength and power in recognizing that we/they are the majority population in the world. By using these various terms, however, I do not mean to imply that they are fully interchangeable with each other. Indeed, lumping people with diverse lived experiences together into any category is problematic. I use more specific references to race or Indigeneity when it is necessary to describe a particular situation or experience, and when it does not reveal the identity of a colleague.

Consistent with Latin American liberation psychologies, I italicize Spanish and Portuguese words. Additionally, I ground this book in my own *vivencia* (lived experience) and *cotidiano* (everyday realities), and I use *testimonio* to tell stories of my own experience as a leader and as someone who follows others. I also share stories in this book to bring to life the concepts of liberatory leadership. Some stories focus on liberating moments, including missteps and successes. I also share stories of oppressive leadership and offer ideas for how leaders could have behaved differently to advance liberation. When I am involved in the story, I own it while also preserving the anonymity of others involved. I have changed the details, including names, in stories that were shared with me or situations I witnessed to protect the privacy of others. Sometimes, these stories are a composite of experiences if these changes are not sufficient to protect the identities of those involved.

There is a universality to the stories. Yet I also acknowledge that any claims of a universal solution—one way to "do liberation"—bend toward imperialism and coloniality. Decolonial and liberatory practice reminds us that each leader's experience is unique given their life experiences, role, and institutional and community context. What works for one leader with a particular title at one institution may or may not work for another. Nevertheless, storytelling is liberating because it dispels the isolation imposed on us, especially those of us with marginalized identities. Sharing stories empowers others to claim a new reality.

Concluding Thoughts

This book is meant to outline liberatory methods for practicing higher education leadership. Leaders who adopt this practice can more effectively cocreate academic environments in which people can be free to contribute their gifts and have fulfilling careers. Throughout the book, I follow the style of this introduction by using scholarly work bolstered by personal experience and practical advice. The goal is to transform our workplaces into spaces in which everyone can thrive and do their best work, without the harm and trauma that come from internalized and enacted oppression. This requires self-liberation, accompaniment, and action, so each chapter concludes with a set of questions to support our collective work to effect institutional change. These questions can be used by individuals, by accountability groups, or with a coach. My hope is that the questions spur readers to cocreate a new academia.

Questions for Reflection and Action

- What excites you about a liberatory approach to academic leadership?
- What aspects of a liberation mindset do you feel most comfortable with right now?
- What aspects of liberatory leadership unsettle your beliefs about leadership?
- Have you observed leaders engaging in elements of liberatory leadership? What attitudes or behaviors did these leaders practice?
- How are you hoping this book will support your leadership development?

CHAPTER 2

Crafting a Liberatory Personal Mission

As I approached midcareer, colleagues became more familiar with the quality of my work. Increasingly, I was asked to serve in various leadership positions; to chair this or that committee or working group and to apply for leadership roles. It was flattering to be sought out and trusted by my peers and supervisors. I said yes to most of these opportunities. It took me a few years to realize that I was allowing other people to make decisions about my future. I began to wonder whether it was wise to wait for opportunities to come to me. Perhaps there were other projects, roles, or types of work that I might want to pursue. It was a confusing time because many things seemed interesting and worthwhile. As I began to ponder these questions, I was fortunate to receive two pieces of advice from Black women leaders. Shirley Malcom of the American Association for the Advancement of Science, on a bus to a National Science Foundation conference about diversifying the professoriate, advised me to think of what only I could uniquely do. She counseled me to leave the rest to others. Another mentor, an HR leader at a university who became my coach, asked me what I valued and found most important about my work. Both pieces of wisdom helped me narrow the field enough so I could choose with greater intentionality. I was able to identify both what I truly wanted to do and what I could uniquely do. With this clarity, I wrote a personal mission statement that articulated my purpose and made it easier for me to chart my path of liberation.

Most higher education institutions have a mission statement. Marjorie Hass (2021), president of the Council of Independent Colleges, explains that an institutional mission and vision is a reflection about what is great about the college or university. She provides a series of questions and creative reflections to spur thinking about one's institutional mission. These questions tap into what your institution is best known for, what aspects of your institution inspire others, and what keeps leaders up at night. Institutional mission statements help guide the work to be done, including how human and fiscal resources are directed.

Whether we know it or not, each of us also has a personal mission. Unlike an institutional mission, which focuses on the work that an institution does, a personal mission sets expectations for how you choose to spend your time and resources across different domains of work and life. Our personal missions capture our imagination and drive us forward. They provide purpose and energy to keep going and the wisdom to stick it out or shift direction when needed. They remind us of what we value, why we do the work we do, what gives us life and energy, and when it's time to rest.

My own mission has essentially been a liberatory one, but until I explicitly named it, I often lost sight of it. I would reach the end of the day or week and realize that I had spent my precious time on nonessentials instead of the things that really mattered to me. For many weeks early in writing this book, I got lost in what appeared to be more urgent needs at work and home. I neglected to set aside time for writing, even though writing supported my goals of personal and collective liberation. We've all fallen into patterns like this. Our missions help us redirect our course and get back on track. In this chapter, I review how a personal mission is foundational to liberatory leadership and I describe the personal work we need to do to craft a critical and values-based mission.

How a Mission Can Liberate Us

Many of us have lost our connection (or never fully connected) with our purpose because of the effects of personal and collective trauma and oppression. The global pandemic, racial injustices, war, and climate change are just a few stressors that have weighed on many of us. Then there are the concerns of life, including caring for ourselves and others. At work, there are the routine demands that take time and the more stressful ones that draw on our emotional reserves. A lot is being thrown at us. This situation is particularly challenging for faculty and staff of the global majority, women across races and sexual identities, and others who have experienced exclusion and marginalization because they are also called on to support marginalized students and colleagues while themselves directly experiencing racism, sexism, and other oppressive actions.

Whether we acknowledge it or not, oppressive culture is designed to keep us busy so that it is difficult to recall our liberatory mission. White Supremacy Culture, for instance, shows up as a felt sense of urgency, perfectionism, and reinforcement of productivity (Jones and Okun, 2001; Okun, 2023). Cultures like this are designed to keep us too overwhelmed to resist. Oppressive cultures also try to rob us of our connection with the people, things, and activities that sustain our well-being and provide meaning to life. It can feel like there is no time to reflect on our purpose, let alone pursue activities that are aligned with it. Making time and space to reflect on and articulate a liberatory mission is itself a form of resistance. And creating a personal mission also helps us appraise the risks and rewards to stay on track. Articulating a personal mission statement derived from the explicit naming of liberatory values provides the foundation for liberatory praxis. To do this, we need to first develop our critical consciousness.

What Can I Uniquely Do?

From a liberation psychology perspective, we are not simply a bundle of personality traits and individual preferences. We are much more, including our historical and sociopolitical context of oppression and liberation. Building a critical awareness of who we are in context is often referred to as conscientization or critical consciousness raising (Freire, [1970] 2000). Conscientization includes the praxis of reading your life—the people and events that predate your existence, your own personal history, and contemporary reality—to learn how oppression and liberation have contributed to your story and your current values. Feminist liberation theologians Elizabeth Gandolfo and Laurel Potter (2022) report that critical consciousness raising among the Comunidades Eclesiales de Base led to an epistemic delinking from colonial ways so that community members could creatively explore fresh ways of knowing and being. Similarly, liberatory academic leaders can delink from oppressive ways if we come to terms with reality. With this knowledge, we are then able to choose actions that are aligned with our values of liberation.

A first step in critical consciousness raising is to inspect our own histories. With curiosity, ask questions and interrogate your experiences to learn the ways in which oppression and liberation have shown up in your family and cultural history. Explore the extent to which forms of oppression have played a role in the lives of your ancestors. In my own process, I have come to learn how these oppressive systems have shown up in both sides of my family history. For my family in Puerto Rico, Spanish and American coloniality, imperialism, slavery, and extractive capitalism created conditions of poverty and dependence that led to family separation, chronic illness and malnutrition, and patterns of migration to the US mainland. These conditions also reinforced a patriarchal power dynamic that oppressed women like my mother who would have benefited from going to college. Coloniality and imperialism show up differently for my father's family from Spain. At an early age, his father worked on steamships that profited from global shipping, made possible by centuries of imperialism. After a fascist dictator took control of the country, poverty in his rural seaside town increased. It became more attractive to leave as, one by one, family members immigrated to Argentina, Cuba, and the United States. My parents' attitudes and values were shaped by centuries of change, their family dynamics, and their own temperaments and personal experiences. I, in turn, am a product of this context. In addition, I continue to be shaped by my choices and their consequences, by my interactions with others, and by the contexts in which I live.

Coming to terms with reality has helped me to interrogate my values. Some may appear to be good on the surface but are instead misguided or self-serving at the expense of my own and others' freedom. This can happen to leaders with one or more dominant identities, no matter how many marginalized identities they also hold. When we ignore our reality, we risk overlooking how we make choices that maintain our own power and privilege when we own individual accomplishments without crediting the systems that permitted or increased the likelihood of our success. For instance, earlier in my life, I prided myself on how quickly I achieved the so-called American Dream for my family. My dad did not finish high school after immigrating to the United States and here I am, a woman with a doctorate! Later than I like to admit, I learned that the "land of opportunity" was built on genocide, settler colonialism, and white supremacy, which enabled my father to find opportunities and allowed me to pursue an education. Yes, I worked hard, and so did my dad, but we had many privileges that eased the way for us. Coming to terms with reality means I can identify how oppression and liberation have shown up for my ancestors and for me.

Learn Your Story

Coming to terms with reality requires that we engage in thoughtful introspection and ask questions such as, "Who do I come from?" "Who made it possible for me to be here right now?" and, "What oppressive and liberatory forces were a part of the histories of this society, the lives of my ancestors and families, and my current community?" This historical exploration may require you to ask questions of relatives to learn more about your family history. Ask for their stories of immigration and migration, as well as their histories of wealth, poverty, and land ownership. Explore the reasons why your family moved and where they moved to; whether they had a real choice about where they lived; why they feel rooted in a particular place; why they changed or abandoned religious or spiritual traditions; and why certain family traditions are celebrated. Listen closely to family stories about hardship and struggle, sifting them for hidden or unacknowledged privilege as well as creative and life-giving resistance. If you are adopted or are estranged from your family, attempt to understand your experiences in the context of what you know about your biological, adoptive, and chosen families or cultures. In addition to relying on oral histories, it may be helpful to delve into historical accounts of your ancestors' experiences. For instance, reading about the Spanish Civil War and colonialism and imperialism in Puerto Rico and Latin America helped me make sense of attitudes and values my parents held and transmitted to me.

Also pay attention to how your historical context manifests itself in your personality and individual choices. Rebecca Pope-Ruark (2022), in her book *Unraveling Faculty Burnout: Pathways to Reckoning and Renewal*, notes that many women who self-select into academia have perfectionistic and overachieving traits. If this sounds like you, it may be worth examining how these traits might have been reinforced by caregivers, teachers, and people in the wider society who knowingly or unwittingly upheld oppressive norms. In my case, my parents invested a lot in my education, in part, because of the poverty and discrimination they experienced. They viewed education as a path to prosperity and freedom for their daughters. I, in turn, did not want to disappoint them. Holding on to the value of hard work and academic success without examining the way historical reality shaped my parents' and my behaviors would have been a recipe for burnout. Recognizing these forces, however, helps me let go of values that are, in fact, oppressive so I can choose a more liberatory path.

Recognize how you have benefited and continue to benefit from oppression in society and at your place of work. Another way to put this is to consider the power and privilege you hold. In higher education, power and privilege can come from positional authority such as a leadership title, full professorship, doctoral degrees, and job security in the form of tenure or tenure-like status. Pre-employment or other experiences with an institution and its employees, such as being an alum or donor at your current institution, or having parents or family members who were employed at a college or university, are more subtle forms of academic privilege that provide insider access to norms, information, and contacts. Power can also be derived from oppressive systems that operate in wider society, such as racism, sexism, ableism, and classism. In addition to identifying the power you hold, consider the extent to which you have upheld the status quo by attempting to preserve your positional power or authority by hoarding decision-making, by voting in ways that serve you and people with similar types of power and authority, or by doing nothing, thereby preserving the status quo.

Reflect on the extent to which you have used your power and authority, no matter how limited, to engage in creative resistance, disengagement from toxicity, or advocacy for and with others. Or perhaps you possess strengths or skills because of your experiences of marginalization and exclusion. After a gathering at my home to celebrate the successful dissertation defense of one of our graduate students, a Latina undergraduate remarked that she felt at home in my lab and working with me. The party underscored her experience. I had invited all the students in my lab, as well as their partners and families. There was music, food, and laughter. It all felt familiar to her. Upon further reflection, I realized that I had cultivated an atmosphere that was similar to the vibe at family gatherings growing up. My lab was about doing science in community and enjoying ourselves in the process. Acts like this protected my students and me from the academic expectation of rugged individualism and competition. (Box 2.1.)

But be wary of falling into the trap of hiding behind your marginalizations. Gloria Anzaldúa ([1987] 2012) reminds us that oppressions are fluid. They can change over time, and we may feel and experience exclusion, discrimination, or marginalization in some environments but not in others. The slippery nature of oppression means we sometimes do not realize that we contribute to oppression by focusing only on how we are oppressed. We try so hard to protect ourselves from the pain of realizing our

---

Box 2.1

Questions to Ponder About Your Story

- Whom do you come from?
- Who made it possible for you to be here right now? To have the life you have?
- What oppressive and liberatory forces were a part of the histories of this society, the lives of your ancestors and families, and your current community?
- How have immigration, migration, colonization, wealth, land ownership, and spirituality factored into your story?
- In what spaces do you have more or less power, privilege, and authority? Why?

---

privilege that we ignore how much power we truly have. I have encountered quite a few professors with dominant identities (usually white, male, or both) who have weaponized their marginalized identities against others with less power. In one case, a faculty member claimed that a male staff member engaged in gender discrimination when he denied a request she made. She had no idea that a supervisor had endorsed his decision beforehand on policy grounds, nor did she acknowledge her power or authority as a white tenured professor making a claim against a staff member of the global majority without tenure. It takes humility and courage to face when we have ignored or, worse, abused the power of our dominant identities or positions. Yet critical consciousness requires us to engage in honest reflection. One way to do this is to recall the times we have pointed to a perceived injustice against us in a way that obscures our relative power in the situation. For instance, if we are white or male identifying and claim we have been oppressed by someone with less positional authority or with other marginalized identities, it could indicate that we are trying to hold on to the benefits we have come to expect from our positions of relative power. As Paulo Freire notes, "An act is oppressive only when it prevents people from being more fully human" ([1970] 2000, 57). Sometimes what we initially interpret as injustice is actually an invitation to become more fully human by releasing attitudes that keep us committed to oppressing others.

Tell Your Story

Once you have dug into your historical and contemporary reality, it is time to pull it all together into a story. The Latin American liberation method of *testimonio* can be a powerful way to deepen your conscientization and engage in collective learning with others. *Testimonio* is a form of oral storytelling that grounds one's experience in the reality of our political and historical situations as well as our hopes for a better future. In *mujerista* liberation psychology, which takes a feminist Latina perspective, *testimonio* offers a more accurate self-definition, cultivates community, allows people to realize that their struggles are not theirs alone to bear, brings out into the open oppressive systemic and historical contexts of colonization and collective resistance, and offers storytellers the support and hope for a decolonial and liberatory future (Fernández, 2022; Comas-Díaz, 2022). It counteracts the silencing and forced forgetting in oppressive environments that suppress corrective action (Gandolfo and Potter, 2022).

Moving from an individualistic storytelling style to one of *testimonio* is an iterative process. For instance, a few years ago, I would have centered opportunity and success in my story. I would have said that I was a woman, Latina, first-generation leader who has had a successful research and leadership career. I've mentored and sponsored the next generation of researchers, clinicians, and leaders. I have overcome obstacles and shown persistence to earn my success. A narrative like this might be inspirational to some, but it does not acknowledge the shared context of my challenges or the costs of my success. A story that stops here may lead me to value hard work and persistence, which may be positive, but it also does not tap into liberatory values of cocreating new definitions of success for and with others who might not have experienced the privileges I had.

Practicing *testimonio*, I have come to understand myself in the context of a long line of women who have resisted oppression. I have learned from my ancestors about how I can resist oppression now and contribute to greater freedom in the environments into which I enter. As I shared earlier, my mother, with whom I was very close, experienced a number of early separations from her family of origin because of her caregivers' premature deaths and her resulting migration from Puerto Rico to New York. Her own mother, a healer in her village who used herbs to treat a variety of illnesses and served as a midwife, died when my mother was only nine years old. My mother's familial trauma was an unfortunate but common by-product of colonization, sexism, racism, and poverty. But because of these experiences and a history of resistance among women in her family, my mother was a relationship healer, always urging others to reconcile and forgive. This role helped the family maintain connections even as the diaspora and separation continued, with relatives moving farther away from each other on the mainland. She also encouraged my empathic tendencies as a child, along with a love of learning, so it is not surprising that I later pursued a clinical psychology degree and became a professor specializing in family and health psychology. And within these fields, I focused on empathy and validation of suffering as key factors to healing. It is no accident that I pursued this path of healing. Yet this journey was not without struggle because of who I am and how I approached my work. For instance, as a researcher pushing back against a dominant medical model that dehumanized people who were suffering with illness, I once received this feedback from a peer reviewer: "This author is setting the field back 50 years!" In fact, I was probably "setting the field back" even further by tapping into methods of healing that existed before colonization. When I reflect on this story, I am more grateful for people who labored before me and for me and their efforts to build community and freedom. I appreciate my responsibility to create liberatory conditions for others as something that began before me. Through this kind of reflection, I am also grateful for the responsibility rather than crushed by it. I am strengthened by the legacy even as I am thwarted.

This sample of *testimonio* provides a glimpse into how critical consciousness might unfold in the act of telling our stories. When I share my story with others, I receive feedback that shapes me still more. Listeners may validate my experiences, ask questions that cause me to delve deeper, and share their own stories that help me see the bigger picture. As I continue to learn and reflect, I reveal my connection to the past and future through my mission. Who I am leads me to think about who I want to be and what risks I am willing to take in the struggle for liberation.

Pay Attention to Your Feelings

Critical consciousness raising will inevitably elicit a range of emotions: joy and gratitude, sorrow, anger, and defensiveness among others. Realizing how we benefit from oppressive systems including coloniality is an affective process (González Stokas, 2023). Anzaldúa, in *Borderlands/La Frontera: The New Mestiza* ([1987] 2012), describes the borderlands as a place of ambivalence and struggle. Anger, shame, and feeling lost and confused are par for the course as we learn about ourselves and our histories. We may rage at the systems that have prevented our ancestors and us from living fully and still love ourselves and others who struggle on (Gandolfo and Potter, 2022).

As you work on your story and share your *testimonio* with others, you may be visited by an enemy of critical consciousness: defensiveness. Defensiveness typically arises when we come face-to-face with the ways our ancestors or we have resisted liberation and supported oppression. Ruchika Malhotra (2022, 26) offers a reminder that may help you remain open to learning: "The problem isn't men, it's patriarchy. The problem isn't white people, it's white supremacy. The problem isn't straight people, it's homophobia. Recognize systems of oppression before letting individual defensiveness stop you from dismantling them."

Liberatory leaders take time to process the emotions that arise as we learn more about ourselves in context. Rely on methods that work for you or try something new, such as spending time with nature or loved ones, journaling, and creating art or music. Also consider sharing your story and your reactions with like-minded others who are on a similar journey of liberation.

Critical consciousness raising is a lifelong endeavor. The process of peeling back the layers to understand ourselves in history and our ever-changing present is never complete. This is not a reason to be disheartened. Rather, it is a hopeful way of living to know that we can always learn something new or more true about ourselves. It also helps us get better in touch with our values.

What Do I Value?

Once we have a basic understanding of who we are, we can consider our values, or how we want to show up for others. Values act as a compass to guide our choices and behaviors. They help us stay true to a liberatory purpose. With a little work, we can articulate our values into personal mission statements.

Values Identification

A quick search online for "values list" results in many hits that can be helpful to consider a wide variety of values that drive us. You may wish to pay close attention to words that represent liberation and freedom to you. Write these values down. They may become part of your personal mission statement.

An additional way to identify liberatory values is to recall the mentors, role models, or leaders you admire and respect for their liberatory work. Judging from their actions, what do they value? What words or phrases do they use to describe themselves, perhaps on their social media profiles? What words can you borrow from them? Reflection of this sort can generate ideas to integrate into your own mission statement.

Your own somatic and emotional experience can also provide important data about your values. It is probably the case that some aspects of your work excite or energize you in your liberatory work. Other aspects may deplete you. When I speak to students, staff, or faculty, I can sense what enlivens them by their upbeat and animated tone of voice and choice of words as they talk about their experiences. In contrast, feeling drained, having headaches and body aches, or feeling dread may indicate a mismatch between values and either the working culture or the work itself. Observe your body and emotions as you go about your day or during a daily reflection time to learn more about where your deepest values reside.

If tuning into emotions is challenging, rely on another person as a sounding board or mirror. Choose people you trust to provide honest and candid feedback about what they observe about your leadership. Ask them when they have witnessed you at your best when it comes to accompanying others in solidarity, speaking up courageously, or advancing policies or procedures to create working environments that are more free. When have they observed you experiencing joy or positive energy? Their responses can help you identify what matters to you most, and whether you are living in a way that fosters freedom for yourself and others.

An Exercise to Connect with Your Values

A creative way to reconnect with your values is to use your imagination. In one exercise, which is practiced in several spiritual traditions and incorporated into some psychological therapies, one imagines attending their own funeral. For those who have experienced trauma or a recent death of a loved one, an alternative is to imagine one's own retirement or going-away party. In your imagination, invite people you know across different life domains to see you off. To encourage a liberatory mindset, make sure to invite people across identities, including with marginalized identities or less positional power than you. Each person gets up to say a few words about you. The question is not, "How will people remember me?" but "How do I *want* people to remember me?" This slight change of phrase helps direct us to aspirational values that we may or may not be living out right now. What do you want people to say about how you accompanied them, supported their growth, empowered them, or collaborated with them to create liberatory systemic change? This is an exercise to return to over time as you uncover the things that matter to you. What you record will indicate your values, which can then be integrated into a personal mission statement. It can be quite motivating to compare our values with our actions, and in fact, critical consciousness demands that we don't stop at reflection but that we act. (Box 2.2.)

Box 2.2

Questions to Ponder About Your Values

- What words signify your values?
- What characterizes the actions of respected mentors or role models?
- When do you feel most energized? Is that feeling a sign that you are doing something aligned with your values?
- How would colleagues or loved ones describe you when you are at your best?
- What does your body tell you about your values?
- What do you want people to say about how you accompanied them, supported their growth, empowered them, or collaborated with them to create liberatory systemic change?

Reality and Values in Action: Your Mission Statement

The most difficult part of drafting a mission statement is getting straight with yourself about who you are and what you value. Once you have done this work, you can then construct a statement. The following is a simple construction: "I do _____ because _____; I [insert value-laden verbs] to [insert value-laden verb]." Adjectives and adverbs help clarify the liberatory nature of your work, but one to two sentences are all you need for the mission statement.

As I embarked on one of my leadership positions, I wrote the following personal mission statement on my office whiteboard to remind me of my work: "I empower people to fearlessly and joyfully recognize, embrace, and act on their giftedness and dignity in service of others, especially the marginalized and oppressed." I admit it is a bit wordy. But this was the first time I had articulated my mission. Notice that my mission statement could be lived out regardless of my position or role or what I find myself doing any particular day. This mission guides *how* I do my work and *what* projects I choose. For instance, by using the word "empower," I'm not making decisions for other people but creating the conditions for them to make sound decisions and act as they see fit. By including words like "fearlessly" and "joyfully," I indicate that I value courage and joy, as I do the dignity of each human person. "Service" appears because I wanted to create a community that supports one another. Also in my statement is the recognition that those who have been left out or excluded are especially dear to me, which is an articulation of the "preferential option for the poor."

This mission statement saved me from burnout by helping me focus on values rather than get sucked into what Pope-Ruark (2022) describes as the danger of a calling. She writes, "When one has a calling instead of a job in higher ed, no matter how great the job is, it's much easier to slowly give more and more of yourself as you buy into the competitive achievement orientation of the academy and the culture, which will continue to pull more from you in the service of the calling" (85). I compared new opportunities with my statement and felt freer to say yes or no to them based on how well the work aligned with this statement.

Mission statements are not meant to be set in stone. My mission has changed somewhat since the initial draft, but there are consistent elements such as empowerment, community, and human dignity. With greater conscientization and awareness, and coming through the collective trauma of the past few years, I have more clearly articulated that liberation and healing are key parts of my mission. As you continue to live out your mission and deepen your critical consciousness, you will become aware of which parts of your work are aligned with the mission and which are not. There may be unpleasant or tedious parts of your job that need to get done to fulfill your mission. But if you observe that you are acting consistently against your mission and your body, mood, and trusted confidants are echoing the refrain, then you may need to revise your mission or change your direction.

Liberation Metrics

A mission statement is like a compass; it points us in the right direction, but it cannot tell us if or when we arrive at our destination. We can set selection metrics to help us choose projects that are aligned with our missions. I learned a great example of a guiding metric from Linda LeMura, president of Le Moyne College. Before taking a new project on, she includes in her decision-making many of the typical indicators such as institutional needs, but what sets her assessment apart is that she factors in joy as a value. She calls this factor the "LL Joy Index" (LL stands for her initials) (LeMura, 2021). It is one example of how to assess the extent to which we commit ourselves to projects that fulfill us.

Metrics can also help us measure the extent to which we have lived our mission over time. As noted plant biologist and academic leader Beronda Montgomery (2020b) persuasively explains, we cannot risk counting on others' affirmation of our contributions, especially in oppressive academic cultures. We must show up already affirmed to maintain our integrity. Montgomery offers a countermetric that captures her values, which she calls the "B-Index" (B stands for her first initial; Mayuzumi, 2017). This personalized index provides a way to measure

---

Box 2.3

Questions to Ponder About Your Metrics

- What metrics or indicators can help you decide whether to pursue new opportunities?
- What are some success metrics to track the extent to which you are living your personal mission?
- How are your metrics tied to your values and your mission statement?

---

activities, choices, and opportunities against one's own, and not someone else's, values. She writes a periodic progress report based on her own definitions of success. (Box 2.3.)

These powerful examples demonstrate how personalized values-based metrics promote healthy resistance to academic reward structures that violate our integrity and values. It is possible and even necessary to craft an alternative, liberating vision.

The work of critical consciousness raising, values clarification, and mission writing takes time. Consider blocking time in your schedule to reflect and get clear on how you want to live your mission. Whether you connect with your values through journaling or conversation with trusted peers, a coach, or friends and loved ones, this precious time offers insights into who you are right now and what you need to do to be the leader you hope to be for others.

Summary

Who we are today is a result of the choices made by generations of people before us: ancestors and others who engaged in oppressive acts as well as those who resisted and worked toward a liberated vision of the future. When we delve into our histories, we learn more about ourselves so we can get clear on our values and choose our actions wisely. Putting your liberatory mission to work will influence how you accompany others, collaborate with others on creating healthier environments, empower others to lead, and take care of yourself in the face of oppression. You can also use your mission to assess your current workplace. Having performed an in-depth scan of your own personal reality, you are better equipped to scan the reality of your academic environment to assess the risks and rewards of leadership, build a network of allies, and set strategy for cocreative liberatory action.

Questions for Reflection and Action

- Which institutional mission statements speak to you? Are there words or ideas you can borrow for your personal mission?
- What oppressive dynamics in your history get in the way of living your values? What liberating dynamics in your history facilitate your work?
- What practices have helped you learn more about yourself in context (e.g., reading, listening to music, visiting art exhibits, attending cultural festivals, following specific social media accounts, testimonio)? What new methods can you employ to continue your consciousness raising?
- How do you feel when you are living in a way that is (in)consistent with your values?
- Identify a trusted person who knows you well. What words would they use to describe what motivates you to create environments that support liberation and freedom?

- What values emerged from the retirement party exercise? In what areas of your life are your actions best and least aligned with your values? What actions can you take to better align your values and actions?
- What is your personal mission statement?
- Where can you post your mission statement so it reminds you to ground your decision-making and actions in liberation?

CHAPTER 3

Reading Reality to Support
Liberating Actions

Newly appointed to our positions, a white male colleague and I attended an introductory meeting with a faculty governance leadership team. After our introductions, I thought we would begin to strategize how we could all collaborate on faculty and staff development initiatives. Instead, the most senior leader of the team, a white man, proceeded to compliment my colleague on his accomplishments. The senior leader never made eye contact with me and instead made passive-aggressive swipes at my qualifications and my role, going so far as to say that my newly created position in faculty development was a threat to faculty governance. It was uncomfortable not only for me but for others around the table, who looked down awkwardly while he spoke. No one said a word about his behavior at the meeting. I remember looking around the room and thinking, "Well, isn't this interesting?"

For all our talk about higher education being a mechanism for social change and liberation, there are obstacles to living out that mission. In this case, the obstacle was not just an antagonistic leader who was using his power and privilege to draw a line in the sand. It was also the culture of silence that allowed this one person to dominate and attempt to derail change efforts by undermining the only Latina in the provost's leadership team. Had I been more junior or less experienced, I'm sure I would have walked out of that meeting with a severe case of imposter syndrome. Because of accumulated experiences like these, I have learned how to read the reality of different situations in order to spot how oppression might show up or be reinforced in an organization. Reading the reality of this meeting helped me choose collaborators strategically to achieve shared goals in faculty and staff development. While the senior leader was never fully on board with my work and still refused to talk to me directly months later, his active resistance lessened when others on his team participated in and even lauded the work I was doing. It was too politically difficult for him to continue to try to undermine me.

Experiences like this one have taught me a lot about power and authority, who is respected, and how I might work effectively in a new role. Like many of my colleagues who have experienced marginalization and exclusion, I have learned to scan the environment to assess the risks of leadership and build a plan to move forward by attending to the extent to which liberatory and oppressive forces are at play. This chapter describes strategies for reading the historical and contemporary realities of your environment. Reading reality means realistically assessing the motivations of people with whom you work and understanding the norms and regulations that reinforce particular behaviors or decisions. We can read reality in the moment as I did in my example, and we read reality when we conduct reviews of documents to understand processes or prepare for a course of action. We can also read reality by asking good questions and checking in with ourselves to gauge our own reactions in real time.

Across institutional types—private and public; rural, suburban, and urban; community college to doctoral degree granting; minority serving and predominantly white; faith based and secular—learning to read the reality of the environment helps leaders identify obstacles to liberating change so they can confidently choose a strategic path forward with supportive collaborators. Because strategy is highly contextual, it also depends, in part, on the leader's positional power. For example, certain actions may be riskier for a staff member without employment security than for an administrator who can return to their tenured professorship if relieved of their duties. Assessing strategy also includes an honest appraisal of the extent to which one holds identities that have more or less power and privilege, including but not limited to race, sex and gender, sexual orientation, and religion. Thus, questions are included throughout the chapter to support the discovery of information you need to set your strategy and act in your context. While the approach in this chapter is ideally implemented when starting a new position, it can be used at any time to build your liberatory practice and confidently move forward in your leadership. In fact, it is useful to periodically assess your environment as you or others change roles or leave the institution, new people come aboard, and priorities change.

The Power of Curiosity

Reading reality at any institution requires that we turn the same curiosity and keen observational skills we applied to ourselves to our working environment. Plant biologist and academic leader Beronda Montgomery (2020a) offers a metaphor that may be helpful when zooming in on the environment: groundskeeping. Groundskeeping requires leaders to cultivate an environment in which others can grow. In her book *Lessons from Plants*, Montgomery (2021) explains that when a plant is not thriving, good gardeners refrain from blaming the plant for its ills. They investigate how the environment might be contributing to poor health. Perhaps the plant needs more (or less) sunlight, a change to the watering schedule, or nutrients. Like gardeners, liberatory leaders examine the environment with curiosity so they can assess its health and collaborate with others to make liberating changes that create conditions in which others can thrive. The point is not to "fit in," assimilate, or accommodate to oppressive environments. Rather, the goal is to counter and resist exclusion, violence, and marginalization and to create a new, healthier reality in which none of these harmful influences exist. We can only do that if we read our situations accurately.

Begin your environmental scan by collecting a variety of documents that set the tone at your institution: mission statements and strategic planning documents, policies and procedures, organizational charts, budget models and documents, collective bargaining agreements, and faculty and staff handbooks. Your scan will also include surveys, institutional data, and conversations with others. Your job as a liberatory leader is to be curious and ask critical reflection questions, some of which are included in the sections that follow, to shine a light on where liberation and oppression are present.

Mission Statements and Strategic Plans

Mission statements are aspirational; it is the rare college or university that perfectly lives its mission. Yet reflecting on the extent to which mission statements and their accompanying documents—vision statements and strategic plans—align with institutional actions can offer useful information. In particular, strategic plans drive institutional decision-making about the strategies and goals that will be pursued in support of the mission. A liberatory review of these documents offers leaders an opportunity to reflect on the extent to which the institution lives up to its mission, especially with respect to communities that have been oppressed in society and have experienced exclusion from accessing the institution's resources. Relevant actions to review include speeches, sponsored speakers, community engagement activities, and curriculum and program decisions, among other actions. Hiring, retention, and budget decisions are also expressions of mission that are discussed in other sections in this chapter. Liberatory leaders critically evaluate not only whether the activities are aligned with the mission, vision, and strategic plan but also the extent to which the words and actions support liberation and oppression.

Worth assessing along with the mission is the history of the institution. Colleges and universities have a variety of origin stories, yet, as discussed in chapter 1, most of the institutions in the United States were founded in a culture of sexism, classism, settler colonialism, enslavement, and xenophobia. Even if the modern mission is described in a way that is different from the original story, history still matters. Endowments, program prioritization, and faculty, staff, and student demo-

---

Box 3.1

Mission Questions to Ponder

- To what extent does the institution acknowledge its historical reality in its mission statement or elsewhere?
- What institutional actions appear to fulfill the stated mission of the institution?
- What actions or inactions fall short of the mission?
- Does the university live up to its mission for everyone or only a privileged few?
- What aspects of the mission resonate with your own personal mission as a liberatory leader?

---

graphics are rooted in histories of oppression. Do not ignore the history of your specific institution when assessing current mission alignment. While you cannot change history, apprehending the historical reality can help identify where and when intervention may be particularly difficult in the contemporary reality. (Box 3.1.)

Assess Policy and Procedure

Policies and procedures may initially appear dry and boring, but they reveal a lot about how the mission is accomplished, who is listened to, and how disagreements are resolved. Values and norms are also embedded in policy and procedure language. Read these documents with a critical lens to identify the extent to which they support liberation.

Documents that are especially important to review include hiring policies (including partner or dual career programs), guidelines, and practices; promotion, tenure, and sabbatical policies, including advancement opportunities for adjuncts and lecturers; remote and flexible work arrangements; parental and medical leave; access to professional development funds; salary equity, across-the-board, and, if they exist, merit increase procedures; nomination processes for awards; and faculty, staff, student, and board governance documents. Using a liberation lens, review the extent to which these policies and procedures gatekeep or restrict access, compensation, career advancement, and recognition. If your organization is silent on any of these issues, consider what that might mean for people affected by the lack of policy.

For instance, in matters of promotion, tenure, and funding, epistemic exclusion is a common form of gatekeeping that disproportionately affects people of color in the academy (Settles et al., 2021). Epistemic exclusion is evident when certain types of scholarly activity (e.g., peer-reviewed articles in top journals vs. public scholarship), methods (e.g., quantitative methods vs. qualitative methods), or disciplines (e.g., "traditional" humanities vs. race and ethnic studies) are rewarded over others because the long-dominant group, originally white men and now people who continue to benefit from the rigid definitions, decided what was of value. Other forms of exclusion, devaluing, and silencing can show up in these policies as well. It is often the case that promotion and tenure guidelines do not account for the labor of informal mentoring and advising that women, people of color, and other marginalized groups do. With no way to formally document these contributions, they remain invisible in performance reviews. People who are engaged in this work are not recognized or rewarded for their labor and, worse yet, it can appear to others that they are less engaged in their work than they truly are. Resources like *An Inclusive Academy: Achieving Diversity and Excellence* (Stewart and Valian, 2018), *Doing the Right Thing: How Colleges and Universities Can Undo Systemic Racism in Faculty Hiring* (Gasman, 2022), and *Faculty Diversity: Removing the Barriers* (Moody, 2011) contain excellent suggestions for inclusive and equitable practices in these domains. Comparing existing policies with the recommendations made by resources like these can help leaders assess the current state of affairs and identify opportunities for liberating changes at their institutions. (Box 3.2.)

Box 3.2

General Policy Questions to Ponder

- How might policies and procedures reinforce racist or sexist decision-making in academia?
- Were the people most affected by these documents involved in crafting them?
- To what extent is epistemic oppression or exclusion embedded in policies?
- Are there gaps in policy that affect some people more than others?
- To what extent do the policies and procedures reflect best practices?

As you review policies and guidelines, also pay attention to processes that are in place to support people who have experienced harm at your institution. Relying on the principle of "the preferential option for the poor," reflect on whether some people are more exposed or vulnerable than others. For instance, a longstanding one-sided policy at one of my institutions prevented staff from grieving faculty but permitted faculty to grieve staff. This policy reinforced faculty-staff power differentials. Reflect also on whether the mechanisms for reporting complaints about racist, sexist, or other biased behavior are clear and easy to understand. Some institutions even have policies in place for academic harassment and workplace bullying behaviors that do not rise to the level of a civil rights or Title IX violation. In the many more cases of institutions that do not have such policies, use your environmental scan to assess to what extent the institution can hold people accountable for their behavior.

Applying the "preferential option" to policy review can be complicated. After campus protests about the Israel-Hamas war caught the attention of lawmakers and donors, many American colleges and universities quickly updated their protest and demonstration policies. Leaders stated that the changes were needed to create safe and civil learning environments. Yet the policies, many created last minute and behind closed doors, also silenced open, respectful dialogue between people of good will who have different opinions, experiences, and identities. To be sure, this is a complex situation but during environmental scans, leaders must pay attention when it appears that policies pit people against each other, especially when people are from different marginalized groups. (Box 3.3.)

Box 3.3

Additional Policy Questions to Ponder

- Is there a formal grievance process for faculty, staff, and students?
- How often are grievances filed at the institution, and how are they handled?
- Is clear information posted on how, when, and to whom one should report biased and discriminatory behavior (e.g., ombuds, Title IX office, human resources, general counsel)?
- Are some people more exposed by and vulnerable because of (lack of) policy?

Organizational Charts, Governance, and Budgets

Budgeting, organizational structure, and governance are intimately connected. They have in common individual people who have the power to make decisions about how work is done, how it is funded (or not), and who else is involved in decision-making. Liberatory leaders pay attention to how these power structures operate to learn about the oppressive and liberatory forces at work at their institutions.

Organizational Charts and Leadership

Organizational charts are often posted on institutional websites (if not, request one!). Not surprisingly, most charts are arranged hierarchically with the president or chancellor at the top, followed by successive levels of administrators. Faculty and staff may not even appear on some organizational charts. Be aware of the number of levels of hierarchy at your college or university. Amy Edmondson (2018) writes that hierarchical organizations contribute to a heightened sensitivity to power differentials, which, in turn, leads to fear and a lack of openness. Likewise, relational-cultural theorists and therapists Linda Hartling and Elizabeth Sparks (2008, 2010) explain that strongly hierarchical organizations get in the way of building authentic relationships because they emphasize transactional relationship building, power-over or controlling relationships, and the suppression of conflict. This can also mean that people will be less likely to challenge the status quo, ensuring that oppressive norms persist. Leaders may not actively seek out authentic interactions with people several levels below or they may reprimand those who skip the "chain of command." This is not to say that everyone who fills these roles upholds power differentials built into the organizational chart, but the very existence of a deep hierarchy can present an obstacle to relationship building across the institution.

Hierarchical organizations may also reflect White Supremacy Culture and the racialized nature of power. For instance, many hierarchies are characterized by the belief that there is one right way to get things done (through the hierarchy), paternalistic decision-making (by people with positional power), and power hoarding, all of which are features of White Supremacy Cultures (Okun, 2023). Sociologist Victor Ray (2019, 36) describes racialized organizations as "social structures that limit the personal agency and collective efficacy of subordinate racial groups while magnifying the agency of the dominant racial group. The ability to act upon the world, to create, to learn, to express emotion—indeed, one's full humanity—is constrained (or enabled) by racialized organizations." In racialized organizations, whiteness is

Box 3.4

Organizational Chart Questions to Ponder

- How many levels of hierarchy exist in your organizational chart?
- To what extent is the power hierarchy in the organizational chart reinforced by leaders?
- To what extent does your institution treat whiteness as a credential, as evidenced by the identities of leaders who are at progressively higher levels in the organizational chart?
- To what extent does the organizational chart at your institution include Black, Indigenous, and people of color at the highest leadership ranks?
- Are leaders with marginalized identities only found in certain offices (e.g., custodial, food service, student affairs, and diversity, equity, and inclusion but less so in academic affairs, finance, and advancement)?
- What explanations do institutional leaders give for the (lack of) diversity in leadership?
- What efforts are institutional leaders engaging in to diversify leadership?

a credential that influences who gains access to leadership and who is listened to. (Box 3.4.)

Reviewing the data, it appears that colleges and universities in the United States are racialized organizations. The American college presidency is predominantly white and male (Melidona et al., 2023). Approximately 72 percent of presidents identify as white, and almost two-thirds of these are men. In addition, most presidents continue to come from senior faculty ranks, which are also predominantly male and white. The trustee population reflects the same demographics. The Association of Governing Boards of Universities and Colleges (2021) reported that nearly two-thirds of trustees at public and private institutions were men, and almost 80 percent of trustees at private colleges and 65 percent at public institutions were white. Board composition is even more white when minority-serving institutions are excluded from the analysis. These are statistics worth paying attention to, since boards hire and fire the president, who then shapes university leadership through the hiring of provosts and vice presidents.

Relatedly, observe how leadership posts are filled across the institution. As Tina Opie and Beth Livingston recommend in their book *Shared Sisterhood* (2022), pay attention to evidence of continued exclusionary practices such as all-white male finalist pools and comments such as, "It's hard to recruit minority candidates here because they get much better offers elsewhere." Watch for language that signals who is presumed to be qualified. For instance, statements like, "We need someone who has done this job before," may sound reasonable at first until one considers how this privileges white male candidates who are afforded more opportunities in formal leadership roles (Caño, 2023).

Faculty and Staff Governance

Extend your scrutiny of power dynamics to faculty governance structures. Although governance bodies such as senates and unions offer a liberatory antidote to administrative power, the humans who lead these groups are not immune to abuses of power. Consider the issues and people who are prioritized by these governance bodies. I have witnessed faculty governance leaders privilege the needs and desires of tenure-track and tenured faculty at the expense of adjuncts, lecturers, and other faculty. Representation either was not extended to non-tenure-track faculty or it was severely limited despite their membership. In another union that included academic staff, there was a clear hierarchy that signaled that staff voices mattered less. Hierarchies like this reinforce the abuse of power that unions were created to challenge.

In addition to the relationships within the governance body, reflect on policy or practices regarding the collaborations between faculty-staff governance and institutional leadership. How these groups of people collaborate on shared goals may also reveal the extent to which oppression and liberation show up at your institution. (Box 3.5.)

Box 3.5

Governance Questions to Ponder

- How would you characterize relationships between administrative leaders and faculty governance leaders? Collaborative? Combative?
- To what extent do these bodies serve the needs of the entire constituency? Does everyone feel equally represented by the governance body?
- If there are multiple faculty and staff governance bodies, to what extent do they collaborate or have a sense of shared solidarity?
- How easy or difficult is it for individual members to raise issues of concern for discussion?

Budgets

Budgets reflect institutional priorities. More importantly, they reflect the priorities of real people: elected and appointed governing boards, presidents hired by these boards, provosts, chief financial officers, and other university leaders, as well as, increasingly in some states, politicians. Compare their words with their spending decisions.

Devote special attention to how budget, personnel, and office space are allocated to work aligned with liberation, including to programs that promote access to higher education; advance knowledge and skills that prepare the workforce to engage with people with diverse backgrounds; and support a sense of belonging for students and employees who have experienced systemic exclusion and discrimination. Example programs include ethnic studies; women's, gender, and sexuality studies; and Native American studies departments, as well as offices devoted to diversity, equity, and inclusion (DEI); Black, Indigenous, and people of color (BIPOC) and multicultural student and community outreach; and LGBTQ+ centers. Starting in 2023, college and university DEI initiatives have been restricted or barred in a growing number of US states under the guise of protecting students from indoctrination, reverse discrimination, and divisive concepts. Even in states that have not banned funding outright, the insufficient funding or active defunding of DEI and humanities programs reflects the values of the leaders making these decisions. In institutions where DEI and related work continues, leaders of these programs, who are often people who hold multiple marginalized identities, are sometimes forced to compete with one another for recognition and resources, which creates conflict and runs counter to liberatory praxis. This situation also diffuses the impact of their efforts.

Reflect on the extent to which your institution recognizes the added labor of doing liberatory work via salary or other forms of compensation. Consider also whether offices dedicated to systemic change and efforts to ensure belongingness have sufficient budget and personnel to effectively do their work. In a survey of chief diversity officers in higher education, Kevin Swartout and colleagues (2023) found that a third had annual operating budgets less than $39,000. Almost half (44 percent) had zero to two full-time employees to lead DEI across the institution. Inadequate investment like this is more telling than the words many institutions use to say they value the contributions of historically excluded and marginalized groups.

Institutional budget models may guide many of these decisions. Some institutions use a centralized budgeting model in which fiscal decisions are made by the president, the chief financial officer, board members, and other senior leaders. Responsibility center budgeting (Curry, Laws, and Strauss, 2013) is used at many institutions as a decentralized strategy that allows deans and unit heads to allocate resources based on their ability to generate revenue through credit hours (tuition dollars), grants and contracts, and benefaction. Most institutions use a blend of centralized and decentralized models. It is useful to know which model is used at your institution to plan how to go about funding new and ongoing initiatives. It is also helpful to pay attention to how the model is implicated in funding decisions. For instance, a focus on revenue-generating actions that are not aligned with the stated mission or values of the institution is cause for concern.

From a liberatory perspective, be wary when leaders rely on "market forces" as an explanation for changes in programming or resourcing. It is certainly true that many institutions must grapple with budget deficits and make hard decisions about resource use and allocation. Yet an overemphasis on capitalistic language is likely to result in decisions that are unilateral, top-down, and contradictory to valuing the efforts of everyone. For instance, "the market" is often blamed to justify the diversion of resources away from programs that are not currently revenue generating. Many colleges and universities have closed humanities and social science programs that are perceived as "unprofitable." In many cases, it appears that leadership did not attempt to educate families and communities about the benefits of these areas of study for building a more just society or the skills that students learn in these programs that will serve them well in their careers and lives. Another example is when salaries in the arts and humanities are significantly lower than STEM faculty salaries despite equivalent workloads. Leaders contribute to oppression when they use "the market" as an excuse for differential pay depending on the discipline.

When leaders use market forces to justify their decisions, they foreclose conversations with their community members and make it seem that the decision is out of their hands. From a liberatory standpoint, these explanations lack creativity and the belief that *otro mundo es posible* (another world is possible). Liberatory leaders observe the extent to which resource decisions are driven by market explanations. They also examine whether decisions are made based on the promise of related benefits such as revenue, fundraising, and political support. (Box 3.6.)

Box 3.6

Budget Questions to Ponder

- How do recent budget decisions signal the values of leaders across the organizational chart?
- How is the community involved in budget decisions? Or are decisions concentrated in the hands of the few?
- Is there sufficient funding for offices and programs that address belongingness, access, and knowledge advancement pertaining to marginalized populations?
- Are "market forces" used as the primary rationale for budget decisions?

Surveys and Data

Climate and employee satisfaction surveys provide high-level information about institutional culture. Request results for groups of individuals who have experienced marginalization and exclusion, especially those who have experienced intersecting systems of oppression. Simply examining aggregated results can obscure differential experiences of climate. If the very small number of people with multiple marginalized identities precludes the release of their results in order to protect confidentiality, you may need to invite members of these groups for individual or small-group interviews to learn about their experiences.

In addition to the results, seek information about the circumstances that prompted the surveys. For instance, some institutions regularly conduct surveys to promote a culture of transparency and action. Others may have been required to conduct a survey because of a crisis or event. In either case, find out how the institution shared the results. Were results released quietly, as part of a public town hall with plenty of advertising, or in some other manner? Learn whether actionable steps were taken to celebrate healthy culture or rectify oppressive or harmful issues raised by respondents.

Data on hiring and retention rates published in annual fact books or posted online can also reveal who feels welcome at your institution and who has access to advancement opportunities. Request trends over time, since publicly available data are often presented as a static snapshot. An institution may celebrate new and diverse cohorts of faculty and staff each year but may not be able to boast an increasingly diverse workforce over time because of attrition. This pattern deserves closer scrutiny to identify the oppressive forces (e.g., epistemic exclusion, cultures of overwork, interpersonal dynamics, racism) that might be at play once people enter the system. (Box 3.7.)

While you are requesting data, also pay attention to how quickly it is shared with you. Resistance to requests or unnecessary delays in the provision of information may signal institutional shame about not achieving diversity goals, paternalistic understandings of equity, or a general lack of transparency. It took one year for me to receive my unit's demographic data, which hampered my ability to track our progress on the institutional priority of hiring and retaining a diverse group of employees. I was told that sharing the data with me would violate employee privacy because there were so few employees of color to start with; I would know who identified as BIPOC. As the first person of color in my role, I was astonished by this response. Not only was I not able to get an accurate read of my workforce diversity so I could begin to learn more about the culture, but I was also blocked from measuring my effectiveness. It took a

Box 3.7

Survey and Data Questions to Ponder

- Who was involved in creating and interpreting the survey?
- What circumstances prompted the launch of the survey?
- What, if any, actionable steps were taken after results were shared?
- What are the barriers to conducting another survey?
- Who are the champions of learning the truth through surveys or focus groups?
- Are hiring and retention rates publicly available? What do the patterns show over time?
- How quickly are data requests fulfilled? What might delays mean?

great deal of advocating to leaders about why I needed the data. This episode also taught me a lot about who had power over data and the overall lack of skill and awareness at the institution. As I describe later, I was able to use this information from my environmental scan to make strategic decisions.

Assess Culture and Climate

Climate can be thought of as culture in action and includes employees' perceptions of their working environment. Since culture and climate are so closely tied, they can be assessed simultaneously and in real time by asking questions and observing people in action. Assessing culture from a liberatory lens requires awareness of the pervasiveness of systems of oppression in higher education. As one of the Universidad Centroamericana martyrs, Ignacio Ellacuría (1990, 183), describes, "In its active sense, culture should strive to establish new values and towards that end it must unmask present values." Reading the culture is one way to unmask present values and systems that are operating in society and in education.

As mentioned earlier, one system that is particularly prevalent in the United States is White Supremacy Culture (Jones and Okun, 2001; Okun, 2023). Higher education cultures can support white supremacy thinking through unspoken norms even while explicitly stating they have no tolerance for racism, sexism, and other systems of oppression. According to Tema Okun, the following norms are characteristic of White Supremacy Culture: perfectionism, a sense of urgency, institutional defensiveness, a focus on quantity over quality (i.e., the production of results is preferred over process), the belief that there is one right way to get things done, paternalism, either-or thinking, power hoarding, fear of open conflict, individualism, primacy of progress, stoic objectivity, and the right to avoid discomfort. These norms exist to some degree at US institutions with vastly different missions and foci. Your job as assessor is to get an accurate read of the characteristics that are predominant at your college or university so you can strategize about advancing justice and freedom for all. Asking good questions in conversation with others and observing their reactions are essential.

Listening Tour Logistics

As Okun wrote with her colleague and mentor Kenneth Jones (Jones and Okun, 2001), "Culture is powerful precisely because it is so present and at the same time so very difficult to name or identify." Leaders need to spend time crafting good questions to expose the culture. One way to do this is through listening tours, which are often recommended as an essential practice for a new leader. Anyone, including those without a formal title, can set up a listening tour to learn more about the environment in which they work. Leaders who are the "first" in their unit (e.g., first woman leader, first leader of color, first LGBTQ+ leader), as well as others who are pursuing the cause of liberation, benefit from listening tours in multiple ways. First, these tours offer an avenue for colleagues to get to know you. The types of questions you ask indirectly and directly signal your values. Second, listening tours offer the leader a way to learn about the real impacts of the mission, the culture and climate, and the policies and procedures at your institution. Third, listening sessions help liberatory leaders identify cocreators and collaborators with whom to build a new reality. Rather than recap the advice about listening tours from helpful books like *The First 90 Days* (Watkins, 2014), let's focus on what is distinctive about conducting listening tours with liberation in mind.

It matters who is on your listening tour. Start by asking your supervisor and colleagues if they have recommendations for a list of people you should include on your listening tour. In addition, ensure your list represents those whose work will be directly affected by your leadership, as well as those who are more "distant" in your organization; the latter may share different perceptions of the institution and your unit. For instance, if you are an academic affairs leader, meet with people in student affairs, event services, financial aid, and other units. Leaders in your town or city are also valuable sources of information. At a meeting with a community leader, I learned that my university was perceived as an inaccessible ivory tower to local people of color. Despite our community-oriented mission and neighborhood programs, we did not actively welcome people who lived in the city onto our campus. This community leader also recommended other people for me to speak with so I could get a more complete picture. She taught me that crowdsourcing my contact list and my questions can result in a richer description of the context in which I found myself.

Although it may seem that an open invitation to chat is an inclusive approach, consider that some people who have had negative experiences with oppressive leaders may not take you up on your offer. They may not trust you yet. Taking a liberatory and trauma-informed approach, it is essential to issue invitations directly to specific individuals, especially to people who have experienced marginalization and exclusion in higher education and in society, including staff and contingent faculty as well as women across races; people across genders who are Indigenous (including Native people with different tribal affiliations), are racialized as Black, or identify as people of color; people from the disability community; and those from the LGBTQ+ community. Whatever your institutional context, consider who might be experiencing greater marginalization due to geographic location, local and global geopolitical context, immigration and citizenship status, and religious affiliation. Include people who are harmed by intersecting systems of oppression to get an accurate read of how oppression operates at your institution. Take care to attend to the racial composition of your tour. A listening tour that primarily includes white faculty and staff, even if they experience other marginalizations, will not provide sufficient information to fully grasp the experiences of BIPOC faculty and staff.

With your invitation, explain that you would like to meet, from a place of curiosity, humility, and support. For instance, "I am reaching out to you because I believe you have valuable insights about working here. I would like to learn more about your experiences so I can be more effective in supporting you and your work." Invite listening tour participants to identify where they would prefer to meet. Some people might feel threatened by getting called into a leader's office. At the same time, it may be safer for some to leave their office for a meeting with you so they can be assured of privacy. Still others may prefer a telephone or video meeting depending on their personal circumstances (e.g., caregiving responsibilities, social anxiety). And others may prefer to meet in small groups because it feels safer to be in community with others who have shared experiences. Offer choice to support the agency of those from whom you would like to learn. Express gratitude for their time and candor both in person and in writing. You may even receive gratitude in return for taking the time to listen. (Box 3.8.)

Our queries may trigger sensitivity in others, especially if we embody change through our lived experiences as a minoritized person. For instance, people may respond with defensiveness or wariness if they perceive your questions as judgmental of norms from which they benefit. Choose open-ended questions that signal curiosity and a desire to learn more. Good starter prompts for listening tours include the following: "Tell me what you love about working here," and, "What are some things that get in the way of doing your best work?" Other questions about mission alignment, culture and climate, and organizational structure and budget are offered in the next section.

Box 3.8

Listening Tour Questions to Ponder

- Do the answers to your questions vary based on the roles of or levels of power and authority in the respondents?
- Do the answers vary based on the identities of those you spoke with?
- Were there common themes raised across listening tour participants?
- What do the answers tell you about liberating and oppressive forces in the unit and the wider organization?
- Who embraced your questions nondefensively? Was anyone offended or threatened by your questions?

Listening Tour Assessment

As activist and author Gloria Anzaldúa ([1987] 2012) notes, oppressions are fluid, so it is important to ask similar questions across people. Collect information about how liberation and oppression show up for different people in different parts of your institution. Notice patterns in responses that vary based on positional power and identity. The responses you receive, along with your liberatory reading of documents and data, will inform your reading of the reality at your institution and help you strategize about your next steps.

In addition to the general questions, test your reading of documents and data by asking questions about other people's responses to these materials. For instance, you might query your listening tour participants about the mission statement: "What is most compelling to you about our institutional mission?"

Box 3.9

Listening Tour Reflections on Mission

- What aspects of the mission resonate with others and why?
- Are there common phrases used to describe the mission? What do they mean to different people?
- Is there a sense of shared mission or cherry-picking of the mission to suit one's own purposes?
- How does your reading of the mission compare with others'? If it is different, why?
- To what extent can people locate the liberating or oppressing elements of the enacted mission?

"What do other people say about the relevance of our mission?" or, "How does the mission guide your work?" Incorporate queries about how the community lives up to aspirations of the institutional mission and whether they think the mission should be amended or revised. (Box 3.9.)

Pay attention when different people across campus repeat the same phrase or use the same words to answer your questions. Do not assume you know what people mean, even if you have been at the institution for a long time. At one of my institutions, for instance, a common response to the question, "What do you like most about our institution's mission?" might be met with, "I love our urban mission." I did too. It was not until my colleagues and I had some disagreements on projects that I realized we meant different things. If I had asked, "Can you tell me more?" or, "What specifically do you like about this mission?" I would have learned that some people loved having access to the variety of cultural and entertainment options in a large city. To others, this phrase meant they loved supporting students from the city who did not have access to opportunities that wealthier suburban schools offered. When people say, "The mission guides everything we do," or give similarly vague responses, follow up to learn whether it is a self-oriented vision of the mission or one that is other-focused.

Workplace diversity and inclusion experts Tina Opie and Beth Livingston (2022) urge leaders to go beyond reading policies; they must also evaluate outcomes. Just because a policy exists does not mean it can overcome other institutional roadblocks. For instance, Opie and Livingston point out that policy effectiveness will be undermined by a culture that discourages critical comments about one's place of work, downplays systemic inequities, or does not analyze and act on data. People will ignore or bend the rules to suit themselves based on these institutional roadblocks. Policies at the greatest risk of being exploited are those that are developed to hold powerful others accountable (e.g., Title IX, bias complaint processes). Find out whether people with different levels of positional power and identities appraise the results of these and other policies favorably. In some cases, you may learn that there is an absence of policy that allows leaders to allocate resources inequitably and without consequences. Or there may be lack of clarity in a policy that permits leaders to make arbitrary judgments that have negative consequences for people with less power. Through your listening tour, you can clarify the actual consequences of policy on people. Similarly, check in with others about how they have experienced decisions regarding new and ongoing initiatives. For instance, in the case of climate surveys, ask their thoughts about the process of developing and launching the survey. Inquire about their impressions of program changes. (Box 3.10.)

Often, conversations about documents, data, and processes yield information about culture and climate that were not evident just by reading documents. At a smaller private campus, I often heard people respond to my questions about procedure with, "We are a relational campus," or simply, "We are very relational." Follow-up questions like, "What does 'relational' mean to you?" "What do you (dis)like about being at a relational campus?" and, "Who benefits from our relational culture?" quickly clarified what people meant. In my listening tour, for some employees, usually alumni and others who had built relationships with colleagues over decades, it meant that they loved the

---

Box 3.10

Listening Tour Reflections on Policy

- To what extent were your listening tour participants involved in developing policies, practices, and procedures?
- Are policies easy to understand and readily available to people across the organizational chart?
- Are there gaps in policies that benefit some people and harm others?
- Are people clear on where to go if they have complaints about racist, sexist, or other biased behavior (e.g., ombuds, Title IX office, human resources, general counsel)?
- If you speak to people who have filed grievances or been the subject of a grievance, were they fairly treated? In their opinion, was due process followed?

---

friendly and welcoming atmosphere. To others, it meant that they needed to know the right colleagues to get something done. For people without social capital, which often meant newcomers and nonwhite employees, there was a clear cost in time and emotional labor to figure things out on their own because of the lack of clear policies and lack of transparency. This type of culture is actually "pseudo-relational" (Hartling and Sparks, 2008, 2010). In pseudo-relational cultures, relationships are key to getting work done and people appear to be nice but are not equipped to manage conflict or challenge the status quo if it means disagreeing with one another. Indeed, I knew how to navigate a culture of nice and benefited from it at times. It was also a roadblock to constructive conflict and healthy change. Had I not asked additional questions or reflected on who benefited from the "relational culture," I might have missed important information about the way the status quo contributed to exclusion in the everyday lives of others.

Of course, it is not possible or advisable to pepper people with every possible question whenever there is a conversational opportunity. Use your judgment to gauge the timing and the depth of your probing during your listening tours. As you establish a knowledge base and develop trusting, collaborative relationships with others, you will get a sense of who is most likely to respond candidly to your questions. Sharing your observations with them can help you and others read the reality as you undertake liberatory culture change.

Observe Others, Observe Yourself

As you go about your business, you will have plenty of opportunities to observe culture and climate in action. Observe how people interact with each other at events and in meetings. Noticing how people engage with each other can teach you about culture in ways that direct questioning cannot.

As you collect information, pay attention to how you feel. We sometimes discount our feelings, not trusting our own impressions, but reading reality requires that we learn to trust ourselves. Your own internal responses to the information you collect can provide valuable information. Indeed, liberation praxis requires that we attend to a sense of knowing that goes beyond words and data. In Latin American liberation and decolonial praxis, this deeper sense of knowing is called *la facultad*. Anzaldúa, in *Borderlands/La Frontera*, writes, "*La facultad* is the capacity to see in surface phenomena the meaning of deeper realities, to see the deep structure below the surface" ([1987] 2012, 60). She notes that people who have been excluded or harmed by others are more likely to develop this sensitivity. Some people refer to this sensitivity in physical terms. I have a friend who calls this sensitivity her "spidey sense." Another refers to this sense as having his "hackles up." (Box 3.11.)

Tuning in to *la facultad* can serve leaders well as they read the reality of their situations. For example, in a group video call with leaders in similar roles, I offered an idea in response to the facilitator's question. The facilitator, who should have known the entire group from prior emails and calls, asked who I was. After I gave my name and affiliation, they assumed I was the interim leader. I corrected them (I was not the interim; I had been in the post for two years). In my gut, I felt like something was not right, but I couldn't put my finger on it. I reached out to a colleague who had observed the exchange. She confirmed that it was disrespectful; it was a microaggression or, to use a more directly de-

---

Box 3.11

Observational Questions to Ponder

- To what extent are participants invited to express their opinions in meetings? Are they acknowledged for their contributions?
- Are leadership hierarchies reinforced by seating arrangements, who is given the floor to speak, or who feels comfortable taking the floor?
- Are people disengaged or acting dismissively? Does it depend on who is speaking?
- Are people actively engaged in problem-solving?
- Are you satisfied with the answers you receive? Is something missing?
- What additional information can you glean from your feelings or your body as you observe others?

---

scriptive term preferred by author Ruchika Malhotra (2022), an "exclusionary behavior." Why does this matter? Trusting my instinct led me to check in with a colleague who had been on the same call to help me read the situation in the moment. Her confirmation helped me make informed choices about how I interacted with this facilitator in the future. If I did not trust my gut, I might have felt embarrassed. I might have wasted energy and time trying to figure out what I did to convey that I was not the "real" leader. Trusting my gut also provided important information so I and others could contribute to liberatory change in the organization.

Put Your Scan to Work

An environmental scan prepares liberatory leaders to navigate their environments to pursue systemic change. So what does one do with all the collected information on mission, values, and culture and climate? A first step is to recall your own personal liberatory mission and how you would like to enact that mission in your current role (see chapter 2 for a review). With your personal mission in hand, examine where institutional mission, hierarchy, policies and procedures, or culture may get in the way of or facilitate your and your team's goals.

Over and Through Obstacles

As you conduct your environmental scan, it is likely that you will discover obstacles to liberating work: inequities and injustices built into the organizational structures and resource allocation, limited power sharing and autocratic decision-making, policies that reinforce inequities or no policies at all, or cultures that silence dissent or invalidate the experiences of already marginalized people. These features of the environment can slow and even prevent efforts to create *un otro mundo posible*. Notice that I do not say that liberation is impossible. This is because liberation and decolonial praxis insists on the possibility of creative solutions, including ones not yet developed.

How you put your assessment of obstacles to work depends on your unique context and goals. For instance, there are actions you can take within your sphere of influence to resist or dismantle oppressive forces in your unit or team. If you manage a budget, consider changes to allocations that permit greater freedom for others to do their work or that can lead to liberating programs or events. With your team, discuss the possibility of modifications to your unit's organizational structure to allow for collective decision-making or checks and balances on your decisions. If you do not lead a unit but you facilitate committees or meetings, consider who else needs to be included to cocreate programs, events, or initiatives that could increase the richness and variety of solutions and so lead to greater liberation. Your scan may also teach you that there is preliminary work to do before engaging in concrete changes. For instance, policies, budgeting processes, or personnel may first need to be created or revised to form a foundation for additional liberating solutions. You may need to build momentum for change by building relationships with colleagues, especially if people are getting in the way of change.

When the obstacle is another person or group of people who are opposing liberating change, assess the motivation. Sometimes, simply educating others about how the proposed work aligns with the institutional mission or with their own goals can be enough to ease the way for something different. It is a bit more difficult to move forward with liberating goals when people with authority and power openly (or not so openly) oppose the work because it is a threat to them personally or to systems through which they maintain power. In these cases, remember that liberation requires collective action and support. One of the benefits of reading reality is that it can depersonalize the situation and neutralize unconstructive emotions like self-pity or defensiveness that could hinder progress. When we remember that the opposition we face is mostly about the change we embody or envision, we can better focus on creatively moving forward with others.

Seek Out Support

More important than identifying obstacles is locating supports to advance liberating change. Some of these supports will be structural, with policies or documents that help clear the way for people to do their best work. Sometimes these supports are not widespread but are found in pockets. In these situations, you can examine how these places of resistance and liberation were born and use them to extend change to other areas of function and other units.

People can also be supports. Supporters include those who are open to learning, share similar goals, and are advancing systemic change of their own. Seeking support is especially important to consider for those with less positional and societal power. Some people on your listening tour might serve as mentors—colleagues who can advise about navigating, harnessing, or changing aspects of the mission and culture. Others can be sought after as sponsors—powerful others who can provide resources or intervene when you are not in the room (Ibarra and Simmons, 2023). Still others may be excellent coconspirators with whom you can cocreate liberating actions. Be on the lookout for allies who may not have the power, time, or energy to actively participate because of burnout, prior workplace harm, fear, or lack of experience. There may be ways for you to include them in the future through *acompañamiento* (chapter 4), modeling courageous action (chapter 5), and growing their skills in leadership (chapter 6).

With your supporters, you can cocreate a foundation for a liberating future. Part of this work involves jointly engaging in critical consciousness raising. Elizabeth Gandolfo and Laurel Potter (2022) state that the effectiveness and longevity of the

Comunidades Eclesiales de Base are partly attributed to communal consciousness raising. Together, community members could read reality and engage in collective action over the long haul no matter the contemporary reality. Note that this is a different approach from the one we typically observe in which leaders, or even a committee or task force, seek input and then make decisions on their own. From a liberatory perspective, reading reality is a communal exercise that results in communal action to solve communal problems.

Strategize and Act

The environmental scan reveals what needs attention. Your reflection on the obstacles and supports to liberating action reveals what and who can help you so you can plan how to achieve collective goals. The questions embedded throughout the chapter were intended to help you uncover the information you need to set your strategy, as contextualized by your positional power, identities, and institutional characteristics. Yet I also understand that having a concrete example can be helpful to show how this can play out. In the following example, I share an experience of strategy and action after conducting an environmental scan in a new position. I also share how I continued to read reality along the way.

One of my responsibilities as a new dean was to diversify the faculty. By reviewing institutional data and existing hiring practices, and in conversations with others during my listening tour, I recognized that it would be meaningful to others if I personally engaged in outreach. So I posted on social media about a faculty opening in a discipline in which women faculty of color were underrepresented. I identified myself as a Latina dean, tagged a Latinx affinity group in the discipline, and encouraged people to apply. Some weeks later, a faculty leader informed me that they had received a complaint about my post; it was perceived as discriminatory. I was asked to seek counsel from human resources to ensure I abided by the law. The human resources department and others agreed that I was simply networking. I confirmed this information with the faculty leader, who then conveyed it to the concerned faculty member. Fast-forward one year. I received another complaint, again through the faculty leader, about a different faculty search. This search had a trained advocate whose job was to ensure that the review and selection process was equitable and transparent (see Stewart and Valian, 2018, and other National Science Foundation ADVANCE work to learn more about search advocates). I had sent volunteers to receive training and then appointed them to departments that either requested an advocate or had little racial diversity among faculty. The search committee members who complained were concerned that the advocate, a tenure-track faculty member of the global majority from another department, was my informant. They reportedly did not feel comfortable discussing the candidates frankly in front of the advocate. In this case, I and others reminded everyone about the role of search advocates, assured everyone that advocates were not spies, and acknowledged that there would be growing pains as we all learned how to conduct more equitable searches, which is what we all wanted in the end.

Through my early scans and a continuous reading of reality, I learned important information about how diversity resistance (Thomas, 2020) showed up at this institution and in my unit. I learned that some people made assumptions about my judgment and competence (assuming I engaged in illegal behavior) or were suspicious of my intentions (believing that the use of search advocates must be a spy technique). A part of our stated culture was to presume good intention in others, but this courtesy was not extended to me when I engaged in liberating work. I learned that my actions and those of faculty of color were scrutinized and demonized in a way I did not expect at this institution given the stated mission. Finally, I learned that the faculty senate was an informal reporting mechanism that was used rather than formal reporting mechanisms for bias and discrimination complaints.

With these observations about culture, policies, and governance, I was able to strategize a way forward. I informed my supervisors how they needed to support me in the work I was hired to do. Specifically, their public and private support could show that my strategies were aligned with our institutional mission. I also invited ideas from my team to resist and oppose the personalizing attempts to dismiss the work we were doing. That is, statements like, "Diversity is personal to the dean," provide an excuse for some to dismiss or undermine values and actions that are shared by the institution and by many others. We connected our goals to diversify the faculty with the mission and provided reminders about our common desire to recruit and retain talented colleagues. We also recognized that the reactions expressed toward search advocates, especially those with minoritized identities, would show up for others engaging in similar work. So we educated advocates to expect suspicion and questioning and reaffirmed our support for them through financial compensation. My team also maintained a good working relationship with faculty senate leadership so that we could quickly listen to and address continued concerns. We collaborated with colleagues across the university, including the chief diversity officer, to underscore the institutional mission and values regarding hiring and retention. I also encouraged colleagues to share how search advocate and other training increased their confidence in running searches with integrity. This was an effective strategy because increasing numbers of faculty and staff sought out the training and volunteered for searches. Across these situations, I admit that I experienced a variety of emotions—everything from anger when I was accused of illegal behavior to joy when I observed successful outcomes. But I was able to harness them in fruitful ways. My personal reading of reality provided good information to start with, and the collective reading of reality with others helped us continue to move forward with confidence even when we encountered pushback.

Summary

Reading reality is a skill that can be applied in any institutional context by leaders throughout the organization. Emerging and seasoned leaders can select strategies and navigate the environment when they pay attention to how oppression and liberation show up in the institutional history and contemporary mission, policies and practices, organizational charts and budgets, and culture. It is strategic to scan the environment through a liberatory lens. Yet strategic thinking is not the only skill that liberatory leaders need to cultivate. They must also develop skills to act empathically and in solidarity with others. Chapter 4 addresses *acompañamiento* (accompaniment), which includes empathic action and solidarity, as a transformational practice to liberate our work environments and ourselves.

Questions for Reflection and Action

- How does your institution's history inform its functioning today?
- How does White Supremacy Culture show up in your institution?
- To what extent does your institution's organizational chart reinforce whiteness as a credential?
- In what way can you imagine yourself as a groundskeeper (vs. a gatekeeper) as you conduct your environmental scan?
- If you were to conduct a listening tour over the next three months, whom would you include on your list and why? Who can help you ensure that your list includes people with diverse lived experiences?
- What words or phrases come up repeatedly when colleagues talk about the institutional mission or culture? To what extent do these phrases mean the same thing across the people you interview?
- When reading the reality of your institution, how can you make use of the information you glean to forge ahead with your work?
- How might you seek support from colleagues and return the favor to accomplish shared goals?

CHAPTER 4

Accompanying Others as a Liberatory Practice

Sabrina was an accomplished scholar and teacher who came to me for advice and guidance. Her department chair recently gave her feedback that she was not doing enough to justify promotion. I listened as she expressed her worries and told of how she had felt undermined by her unit head. We then talked about ways to navigate the situation, including how and when I could advocate for her. Some weeks later, she stopped by to share some updates. She told me that, for the first time, she felt like someone with authority believed her experience. She said it was healing to have been listened to without judgment. I was shocked to learn that other leaders had not extended her the courtesy of listening to her concerns. They counseled her to accept the head's feedback. They minimized her worries; all would be well in the end. They did nothing to ensure just decision-making or due process. These leaders might have felt better after their conversations with Sabrina, but they left her more distressed and anxious about her future, which undoubtedly affected her ability to do her best work. Unfortunately, these leaders missed important opportunities to learn about her situation and the oppressive dynamics that also affected others. They not only caused harm but also missed an opportunity to contribute to a liberating future.

Liberation psychologists Lillian Comas-Díaz and Edil Torres Rivera (2020a, 297) define *acompañamiento* as "an intentional act of being and experiencing social conditions alongside those who are affected by these and interconnected systems of oppression." According to Jesica Siham Fernández (2020, 93), "*Acompañamiento* is being, doing, and feeling with and in the company of others." For Archbishop Óscar Arnulfo Romero and the Jesuits of El Salvador, *acompañamiento* was a form of witnessing to the experience of others; a form of "with-ness." For the Comunidades Eclesiales de Base (CEBs), *acompañamiento* allowed them emotional space to heal from internalized oppressive beliefs and the oppressive actions of others. Accompaniment is central to liberation. It helps everyone develop their critical consciousness to engage in collective action from a place of agency and freedom (Gandolfo and Potter, 2022).

Acompañamiento is more than just a vague sense of solidarity or theoretical empathy with oppressed groups. Accompaniment is a relational practice; we enter into dialogue with real people, often through the sharing of *testimonio*—storytelling that is grounded in reality and centers the perspective of the "owner" of the story. This means that *acompañamiento* requires the companion to offer themselves in relationship to the other, and to allow themselves to feel the weight of oppression even if they have not directly experienced the same type of harm. Companions often experience healing in the process of accompanying others, which is consistent with Paulo Freire's ([1970] 2000) observation that liberation of the oppressed fosters freedom in oppressors as well. Companions are freed from oppressive beliefs about themselves and others so they are better prepared to support and participate in systemic change.

In this chapter, I provide guidance on the practice of *acompañamiento*, including how to build the capacity to empathize with others who have experienced different harms from the ones we have. I also discuss the ingredients of accompaniment, including showing vulnerability to others, listening empathically and nondefensively, and relating to others in a way that centers and validates their experiences. Accompanying others is not limited to dialogue but also requires collective action to rectify systemic harms and celebrate the strengths of others. I conclude with a discussion of how to meet the challenges of accompaniment. But first, let us start by acknowledging that accompaniment is risky no matter who you are.

The Risks of *Acompañamiento*

When we enter into another person's experience, we risk becoming vulnerable. We risk experiencing what they experience: their joy *and* pain. We risk being transformed by the other person. This kind of solidarity, where we draw close to another person rather than standing at a distance, must come from a place of humility and an openness to being changed. This stance requires inner strength and a firm knowledge of who we are in relation to others. Although I have experienced accompanying leaders, I have also witnessed leaders who set themselves apart from others and resisted getting to know others and being known by others. I have also witnessed leaders who cultivate a false sense of solidarity; they appear to accompany others in words but do not follow through in meaningful ways. Leaders who distance themselves for one reason or another are so rampant in higher education that leading with solidarity and accompaniment in mind can be lonely until there is a critical mass of leaders who truly practice *acompañamiento*.

We also risk falling into a savior or hero role when we try to practice *acompañamiento*. If we come at accompaniment as a way to "fix" the system on our own, we risk causing harm through our inauthentic accompaniment. Kim Scott (2021) calls out the trap of becoming a hero or savior when we try to undo toxic workplace culture. We mistakenly believe we will save the day by providing our "generous" help to someone with less power and privilege. Perhaps even more pernicious is when leaders with more dominant identities recognize historical and contemporary oppression but act from a stance of superiority or sense of pity. They take away the agency of others by underestimating their strengths and skills to improve systems. Leaders who do not recognize the systemic underpinnings of individuals' experiences may try to save or fix individuals in their care through a flawed sense of accompaniment that serves the leader's interests. In these situations, leaders risk creating a harmful dependency or alienating others by diminishing their agency. They also uphold the status quo by invisibilizing and shielding oppressive systems from change efforts.

Likewise, if we frame our accompaniment as trauma informed without also recognizing how the system has contributed to the trauma, we risk extending a false accompaniment through trying to fix individuals. As Robin Kelley (2016) points out, "Managing trauma does not require dismantling structural racism." According to liberation psychologist Lillian Comas-Díaz (2020), oppression trauma results from events arising from systemic oppression, not random events. When we fail to consider how a broken system has created repeated trauma, however, we end up pathologizing or pitying the individual.

To manage these risks, we can stay grounded in our liberatory values. Recall your personal mission and how you came to be at this place and time. Check in on your motivations for accompanying others and for jumping in to solve problems. Seek support from like-minded colleagues and trusted people who support your liberatory mission and can accompany you as you learn to accompany others. Remember that every situation, including our mistakes, is an opportunity to learn and grow into your mission. Have compassion for yourself on this journey. With these reminders, let us map out the practice of *acompañamiento* as a leader.

Preparing the Ground for Accompaniment
Build Your Empathic Capacity

Acompañamiento requires that we have foundational knowledge of and empathy for other people's experiences, especially those who have the least power or who have experienced marginalization, similar to the "preferential option for the poor" that was embraced by the Universidad Centroamericana Jesuits, the CEBs, and others. Tina Opie and Beth Livingston (2022) describe a process of learning using dig and bridge metaphors. They write that it is essential for people with dominant and marginalized identities alike to dig into personal experiences, learning, and biases so they can bridge the divide through intentional relationship building.

I agree that, as other writers have recommended (Opie and Livingston, 2022; Malhotra, 2022), reading is one way to build empathy, knowledge, and skill. I have learned about history, culture, injustices, and triumphs by reading novels, short stories, and poetry by Black, Indigenous, and Asian American women. I have also become more connected with my own history and the varieties of the Latine experience through reading and films. The humanities, arts, and music offer myriad ways for us to learn about ourselves and "the other." These disciplines can enhance our ability to pause, check biases and stereotypes, share joy, and take the perspective of others who have lived experiences different from our own.

Many of us can also benefit from reading critical and modern interpretations of historical events we did not learn as children. Books like *An Indigenous Peoples' History of the United States* (Dunbar-Ortiz, 2015), *So You Want to Talk About Race* (Oluo, 2018), *Stamped from the Beginning: The Definitive History of Racist Ideas in America* (Kendi, 2017), *The History of White People* (Painter, 2011), and *How to Hide an Empire: A History of the Greater United States* (Immerwahr, 2019) have helped me understand how colonization, anti-Black racism, sexism, and American imperialism have operated over time, in my own family history, and in the world today. As I consider the *compañera* (companion) I wish to be, books by Indigenous authors such as *Braiding Sweetgrass: Indigenous Wisdom, Scientific Knowledge, and the Teachings of Plants* (Kimmerer, 2015) and *Fresh Banana Leaves: Healing Indigenous Landscapes Through Indigenous Science* (Hernandez, 2022) have also offered a healing blueprint for the restoration of right relationships—between peoples, and between people and the land. I have also found it helpful to follow the social media accounts of historians, sociologists, and political scientists, all of whom have introduced me to new concepts and ways of thinking about gender and sexuality, body size, race and colorism, (dis)ability, religion and spirituality, and intersecting systems of oppression. If you have one or more dominant identities, be intentional about following the accounts of people from historically marginalized communities, especially those different from your own. Do your work to root out your own racist and oppressive beliefs.

Reading *testimonios* can also deepen your empathy for your colleagues. *Presumed Incompetent* (Gutiérrez y Muhs et al., 2012) and *Presumed Incompetent II* (Flores Niemann, Gutiérrez y Muhs, and Gonzalez, 2020), *Women Leading Change in Academia* (Rennison and Bonomi, 2020), *Written/Unwritten: Diversity and the Hidden Truths of Tenure* (Matthew, 2016), articles in the National Science Foundation's *ADVANCE Journal*, and the *Conditional** blog (a blog published by *Inside Higher Ed*, https://www .insidehighered.com/opinion/career-advice/conditionally-ac cepted) offer first-person accounts of injustices faced by women across races in higher education, along with examples of resistance and solidarity to create change. Other sources continue to be published as liberation winds its way through the halls of the academy.

Finally, listen to your friends, colleagues and students, and the members of the community in which you reside. Conduct an analysis of your network to determine where you have diversity gaps. If your network includes few or no people with intersecting marginalizations, figure out a way to bridge the divide and expand your network. For instance, if you are a white man and all the women in your network are white women, it is time to work on cultivating a network that includes Black, Indigenous, and other women as well as nonbinary and gender expansive people of the global majority. The point is not to exploit your network's knowledge or experiences but to work toward "a justice of recognition, whereby each person is appreciated as an intersectional montage, treated with dignity for the various identities and commitments they embody, not forced to assimilate or adjust to oppressive conditions" (Neville et al., 2021, 1253). Be patient, because cultivating a diverse network takes practice, time, and humility.

Model Psychological Safety

Psychological safety—the belief that the leader truly values vulnerability and candor among team members (Clark, 2020)—is highly pertinent for preparing the ground for *acompañamiento*. Amy Edmondson (2018) describes evidence-based strategies for leaders to support psychological safety and offers a short survey that leaders can administer to assess psychological safety in the workplace. Applying a liberation lens by modeling vulnerability and candor, leaders can contribute to liberation from oppressive norms of overwork, toxic self-sufficiency and independence, and stoicism. Leaders can demonstrate that openness is an institutional value that empowers others to come to work as whole human beings.

One way for leaders to model psychological safety is to ask for help. For instance, a colleague of mine who was a new externally hired leader made it a point to ask her department for advice on where to shop and dine in her new city. She also asked for help understanding the norms of how work gets done at the university. Leaders can also model psychological safety by sharing their thoughts and feelings with others, about current events, university initiatives, or their own personal hopes and dreams. But it needs to be authentic, genuine, and personal, not a generic expression of socially expected reactions often found in "thoughts and prayers" messages. One leader I have observed took pride in being hard to read, an enigma. In this person's mind, leaders were benevolent but inscrutable. Others read this presentation as inauthentic, as if this person were wearing a mask. People did not tell this leader what they really thought because they were unsure how the leader would receive the information. It was a futile guessing game that resulted in lack of trust in the leader's true motivations.

There are, of course, legitimate reasons for refraining from disclosing personal information or emotions. You may want or need to protect your privacy. I am also keenly aware that it is easier for cisgender straight white males to be vulnerable, given their default power. Because of gendered norms, men appear to earn more points for disclosing vulnerability. In contrast, expressing certain feelings may be more difficult for women of color and others who have experienced marginalization, because of harmful stereotypes like "the angry Black woman," "the feisty Latina," or simply "emotional woman." It can be difficult to practice vulnerability and courage when one has been subjected to multiple systems of oppression.

At the same time, there are ways to let other people get to know you by disclosing your reaction to shared events. Allow me to share an example. I experienced my first wildfire season just two months after I joined the university as a new dean during the height of the pandemic. Almost all my initial meetings with my new colleagues were via Zoom. During what was a stressful time of transition and social disconnection, time outdoors among the pine trees, rivers, and lakes served as a respite. Then came the wildfires. The smoke plumes brought hazardous air quality that eliminated the ability to spend time outside. I felt demoralized. I also realized that others were probably feeling the same way. So I emailed faculty and staff acknowledging that we were working under conditions that could produce burnout. I also recorded a video greeting sharing how I felt, a bit of advice on focusing on what needs to be done in the moment, and my confidence that this feeling of desolation would not last forever. I hoped that this message would be helpful as people navigated an unusual start to the academic year with ever-changing pandemic guidelines, wildfire smoke, and all the rest that people were dealing with. In response, faculty said that this bit of accompaniment helped them focus. Others said it meant a lot that their dean took the time to record the video; that they felt like their humanity was validated. My disclosure about the impact of the pandemic and the wildfire united with others' experiences. Faculty, staff, and students realized that I was a human being struggling with the same things, that it was safe to feel this way, and that I wanted to accompany them through these events.

Leaders can also signal psychological safety and a willingness to engage in *acompañamiento* through their outreach. Attend events that support communities that have been the most marginalized and excluded at our institutions. Reach out to others through video or social media, curating your messages carefully to indicate you are a leader who accompanies. You will know you are on the right track by how people react. If people who have experienced marginalization respond with gratitude for your message or share how it strengthened them in their work, then you can feel more confident that you are contributing to a safe environment for others. Silence may mean that you need more training in that modality, that you mistimed the message, or that your message fell short in some way. Ask for feedback from trusted colleagues who will tell you the truth and help you improve.

Practicing *Acompañamiento*

Archbishop Romero and the Jesuits of the Universidad Centroamericana are remembered for their *acompañamiento* to the most victimized and marginalized members of their communities. They learned and were transformed by listening. Romero and the Jesuits learned to become keen listeners, in part, through their pastoral training. Even so, it took multiple encounters with community members, including the CEBs, for them to recognize and respond. For instance, early accounts of Romero's ministry show that he initially dismissed the experiences of the oppressed when they pressed for changes that his powerful allies did not want. We can be heartened by the fact that *acompañamiento* can be learned.

Acompañamiento is more than simply adopting a trauma-informed stance that recognizes the widespread nature of trauma that people experience outside the academy and bring to work. As a liberatory practice, leaders also acknowledge that the power they hold can also be an instrument of oppression inside the academy. They are present in solidarity with others and ensure that the workplace is not the site of recurring or new harm, violence, or trauma. Without this awareness, leaders are not able to participate in systemic change that counters oppression. To be in relationship with others requires foundational psychological and interpersonal skills to accompany others without exacerbating existing trauma or causing additional harm.

Mindful Listening

Acompañamiento requires mindfulness, which is a nonjudgmental awareness of the present moment (Kabat-Zinn, 1982, 1990).

When we are mindful, we register thoughts, feelings, or sensations and refrain from judging the experiences we have as good or bad. Because *acompañamiento* centers the experiences of people harmed by exclusion, othering, and other harms, mindful listening becomes liberatory not only for the listener but also for the person being listened to. This type of listening also has roots in acceptance, or a willingness to experience the full range of emotions. To learn to listen in *acompañamiento*, we can take lessons from psychological practices such as Mindfulness-Based Stress Reduction (Kabat-Zinn, 1982) and acceptance and commitment therapy (Hayes et al., 2006), as well as mindful practices across religious and spiritual traditions.

By definition, *acompañamiento* is mindful because we are fully attuned to the other person. There are several ways to show we value our conversation partners with our full attention. We can put the phone and other devices away or turn them off completely. If you need the phone's ringer or vibration turned on or if you need it in view, explain why. Make eye contact if it is welcome and culturally acceptable. Show that you are paying attention through your body language (e.g., appropriate and nonintrusive head nodding, facial expressions, or verbalizations that convey that you are listening but that do not interrupt the conversation flow).

A core practice of the CEBs during the sharing of *testimonios* is that people refrain from interrupting while the speaker shares memories and makes sense of what has happened to them. The community creates a container to allow people to process everything and to digest what is being shared. We can do the same by allowing pauses even after it appears someone has finished talking. They might have something to add. Your receptivity is also demonstrated by refraining from offering an alternative take, turning the focus on something similar that happened to you, or dismissing their concern. Sometimes people will share their anger, sadness, or upset about something you or your team did. This is not the time to defend yourself, your colleagues, or the institution. Interrupting in these ways centers your experience as the more powerful other. Interruptions and counterarguments are especially harmful if you hold more dominant identities than the person who has taken the time to share their pain with you. By attending fully to the other person, you give them the space to experience and process complicated thoughts and feelings, as well as an opportunity to be validated by you. You also benefit from the opportunity to be liberated if you humbly take in what they have to say.

At times, our capacity to pay attention to others is limited because of illness, a rushed schedule, or our own experience of stress and workplace trauma. In some cases, we may have chronic health challenges like chronic pain or attention-deficit hyperactivity disorder, which make sustained attention more challenging. Recognize the conditions and situations that make it more difficult to be present to others. For transient issues, perhaps there is a way to prepare by taking deep breaths or scheduling quiet time before a meeting that will require mindful listening. In some cases, it may be better to reschedule a meeting if you know you will not be able to pay attention. With more chronic challenges, consider disclosing that you may need to move around, take small breaks, or engage in other actions to help you stay focused.

Mindful Attunement to Yourself

Acompañamiento requires that we are attuned to our own inner reactions in response to hearing another person's story, including stories of trauma and oppression. By listening to ourselves, we can prevent our own vicarious traumatization and also monitor our reactions so we do not harm others. To do this, notice the thoughts and feelings that arise as you listen, and be curious rather than judgmental about how you would have responded if you were in their shoes. A common reaction for leaders upon hearing another person's stressor is to think that their listening partner is overreacting. Accept that what might seem like an "out of proportion" response may be a normal reaction to trauma or oppression. Reflect on whether you are judging because the other person's experience or emotions inconvenience you or make you uncomfortable. I once had a coaching conversation with an executive leader about a midlevel leader, a woman of color, who reported to one of his male colleagues. The executive leader told me that the midlevel leader seemed emotionally unbalanced while she talked about how she felt mistreated and undermined by the other leader. If he had taken a trauma-informed and liberatory stance, he might have realized that the midlevel leader had experienced chronic undermining and dismissiveness as a woman in her discipline. He also might have realized that other people were having similarly oppressive experiences with the leader in question. Her emotional reaction was justified given her experiences, and a systemic solution was warranted. If you get the sense that something feels out of proportion, consider why before jumping to conclusions.

Recognize if you have long-standing blocks to listening that need to be addressed through critical consciousness raising, self-reflection, and perhaps therapy. For me, one of many course corrections came through a training program on a life stress interview that I planned to use in my research program. Compared with my peers in the same course, I consistently underrated the severity of different types of stress and trauma. Our trainer said she last saw ratings like mine when she trained a military general. She humorously nicknamed me "the General" for the rest of the course, and I learned very quickly to recalibrate. Between my history as family peacekeeper and a research career focused on intense stressors like infidelity, family violence, and chronic illness, I had learned to protect myself by minimizing the impact of stress in my own and others' lives. If I continued to minimize, I could not live out my value of accompanying others who were suffering. I might be able to listen and say empathic things, but I would not be able to feel the weight of others' experiences. I would not be able to fully participate in liberating transformation. It took some time for me to learn to be more open to the suffering of others in a more authentic and caring way.

If you find yourself shutting down while listening to others—signs like yawning when you got enough sleep the night before, feeling tempted to check or even checking your phone without it notifying you, glancing at the clock—take notice non-judgmentally and reattune to the present moment. These may be indications that you would benefit from further reflection: Do you need more rest? Was the topic of conversation difficult? Why? Might you need more low-stakes practice with loved ones to balance attention to the other and to self? Did learning of the other person's experiences open old wounds of your own experiences of oppression? Take time to consider your own reactions so you can become a more skilled *compañero/a/e* (companion).

Respond with Emotional Validation

We honor the experiences of others when we listen mindfully. But *acompañamiento* does not end with listening; more is required of us. When I worked with people managing chronic pain in therapy, they would routinely report that it was hurtful when loved ones responded by criticizing them, ignoring the pain, or minimizing their distress. In fact, the dominant treatment model at the time encouraged loved ones to ignore the pain so as not to reinforce "pain behaviors" that could lead to further impairment. Similarly, many leaders act as if empathic responses are harmful. In their minds, giving people the time to vent is good enough, but they stop short of validating their concerns out of fear of reinforcing "squeaky wheels" or inviting more complaints in the future.

Perhaps unsurprisingly, my research showed that invalidating responses to distress about pain are harmful to one's well-being and to interpersonal relationships. What people want and need is emotional validation, a mindful response that conveys empathy and an appreciation of the other's dignity as a human being. My colleagues and I described the ideal mindful response as "relational flexibility," or "the ability to interact with one's partner, fully attending to the present moment, and responding in a way that serves one's own and one's partner's values" (Cano et al., 2018, 119). Relational flexibility is fostered through the provision of emotional validation rather than emotionally invalidating behaviors like ignoring, criticizing, and even problem-solving. Taking a page from this research can offer liberatory leaders an opportunity to cocreate trust and *acompañamiento*.

It may seem intuitive to refrain from criticizing others for being targets of harmful and oppressive actions. And yet it happens in academia. Faculty and staff who seek support and *acompañamiento* from leaders have reported to me that leaders instead said, "I wouldn't have done that if I were you," or, "If you decide to go forward with this complaint, it will hurt your chances of promotion." These judgmental responses directly or indirectly criticize the person or place blame on them for systemic oppression. As Kathryn Becker-Blease (2017) notes, trauma-informed care requires that we refrain from blaming and shaming individuals for their trauma. Similarly, statements like, "I totally understand," or, "I know what you're going through," will likely be received as invalidation no matter how closely you can identify with the person. Instead, offer that you have some sense of their experience but that you recognize that their experience is unique and that you want to learn more. Other emotionally invalidating responses might make us feel better in the moment but flatten the experience of the other person. These include minimizing statements like, "You are overreacting," or, "Don't worry about [the situation]—I'm sure it will be fine." Any kind of invalidation elicits less trust and felt psychological safety, undermining leaders' abilities to cocreate liberatory culture change.

It may come as a surprise that problem-solving can also be a form of invalidation. How can this be, when it is often coming from a place of good intentions? The trouble is that we often want to solve other people's problems because it makes *us* feel better. We feel good about helping someone else or fixing the situation. We might also want to eliminate our own feelings of discomfort that arise when we witness another person in distress. No matter the circumstances, jumping into problem-solving before the other person is ready invalidates their experience and takes away their agency. Sara Ahmed, in her book *Complaint!* (2021), describes how premature problem-solving hurts those who have experienced sexual harassment and discrimination. When leaders jump into problem-solving, they may rush to implement problematic policies, inadvertently dehumanizing and demoralizing others in the process.

Rather than responding with invalidation, try empathic statements that affirm or center the humanity of the other person. Such expressions have been central in psychotherapy for years (Rogers, 1946), but they are not specific to therapeutic settings. One way to affirm another person is to extend gratitude: "Thank you for trusting me enough to share these experiences with me." You can also acknowledge that harm was done: "That sounds rough. I'm mad and sad with you that this happened," or, "What an injustice. I'm sorry to hear about this." These can be powerful statements for people who have not experienced *acompañamiento* from leaders before. If you are the one who has harmed the person or if you allowed it to happen, then apologize for your role. This is difficult for many leaders and requires courage because of the ways higher education prioritizes institutional risk management over the well-being and health of its individual members.

As a counter to premature problem-solving, try asking what the discloser wants or needs. When in doubt, questions like, "I want to help rectify this situation. What would you like me to do?" or, "What would you like to get out of our time today?" center the person with less power and allow them to guide the conversation. And whatever you do, be genuine. Words are only one part of the empathy equation—social scientists have shown that our tone of voice, facial expressions, and body language override what we say (Coan and Gottman, 2007; Ekman and Friesen, 1975; and Harvard Business Review, 2017, for an overview of emotional intelligence). If you don't mean it, don't say it.

Empathic Action

Liberatory leaders participate in systemic change by taking action after they listen to and validate others. Perhaps you have observed leaders who give constituents time to express their concerns about a proposal or plan just for the sake of listening. They may even express empathy for others' concerns or fears. But then they take their own preferred course of action, all the while stating that they let others "be heard." Performative listening like this is oppressive and invalidating to those who took a risk to share ideas.

One way leaders can take personal action after engaging in empathic listening is to reflect. They might spend time after the meeting to reflect on their own reactions and consider who else to consult and how to respond. Reflection is part of liberatory praxis because it can result in greater critical consciousness and solidarity. It is wise for the leader to inform others about what may appear to be a delay in visible action. Leaders can also respond in other ways that affirm the people who shared. Thank-you notes, sympathy cards, and messages extending support can change culture from one of silent suffering and isolation to one of *acompañamiento* and appreciation.

Liberatory empathic action also includes collaborating with and learning from others. For instance, upon learning about a harmful problem from one or two people, a leader may decide to widen their listening tour to learn the scope of the problem. They might also decide to invite the people most harmed to participate in revising policies or practices that have affected them. Psychologist Helen Neville and her colleagues call centering those most marginalized in this process the "justice of participation" (2021, 1253).

Stepping back is another form of empathic action. It requires humility and confidence for leaders to let go of the reins and allow others to lead change efforts. Yet it sends a strong signal that the wider community has the wherewithal to contribute to efforts to create healthier environments. It can also be affirming to those who have experienced trauma and harm to carry out this work, if they choose to do so. After hearing from several faculty and staff about rampant academic harassment and workplace bullying, I asked them if they would be part of a task force to create a strategy to improve the culture. They welcomed the validation of their experience but, more importantly, they were energized to take ownership of a solution.

Whatever empathic action you engage in, invite accountability for it. Ask your team what they would like your role to be and share your own ideas. Ask how they will know that you are living up to the standards and goals you create together. Be clear about the measures of success so that together you know if you have met expectations of a leader who engages in authentic *acompañamiento*.

Accompany Others with Joy

Acompañamiento is not limited to times of pain and suffering. Liberation can be found in the ways in which people thrive and find joy (Gandolfo and Potter, 2022), including in celebrating wins and successes. Karlyn Crowley and Jay Roberts (2022) call this nurturing "an appreciative culture." They suggest beginning meetings by having attendees share appreciation for others. This sets the stage for *acompañamiento* during rough times because everyone recognizes that their contributions are valued. We can also nurture appreciation by nominating others for awards, sending notes of gratitude, and asking others to share good news so we can spread the word. We engage in validating accompaniment when we slow down to recognize the efforts of others. It's not just our words that are validating; how we spend our time is also symbolic of validation. We resist grind and overwork cultures when we take time out of our busy days to accompany others with appreciation.

Challenges of Accompaniment

Acompañamiento challenges us as leaders to embrace a different style of leadership from the one that has been modeled in higher education. To accompany others means entering into their experiences and welcoming the opportunity to be transformed in the process. *Acompañamiento* is an attitude we carry as we go about our day. This is a challenge because of the many demands on our time. Yet we can be intentional in creating space in our calendars to be with people. One method that worked particularly well for me as a new leader during the pandemic was to invite groups of people to virtual coffee hours. Some of these were open to all, and some were specific to identity groups (e.g., LGBTQ+) and professional categories (e.g., lecturers and adjuncts). The coffee hours created space for participants to say things they might not have shared in mixed company for fear of reprisal. The time also communicated my openness and commitment to change systems that cause harm. You might be tempted to wait for people to come to you, but recall that there is a power differential that might be a barrier for some people.

Sometimes people who come to us for support have marginalized, othered, or bullied others. What then? Recall that we have a collection of identities, some of which are privileged and some of which are marginalized. This means many of us benefit from oppression in some way even while we experience marginalization in others. It is possible to accompany everyone in a way that supports liberation. For instance, when I have met with faculty because they were accused of saying harmful things to students, I have started by acknowledging their feelings. They may have been surprised, angry, or hurt about the accusation and about my invitation to discuss it, especially if they had never gotten feedback like this before. I admit it was challenging to validate their emotions while also taking care that I did not uphold oppression by validating their racist, sexist, or other harmful actions. In some cases, it took a great deal of effort to listen, mindful of my own inner reactions of anger or frustration, while also compassionately holding them accountable for their behavior.

Not everyone wants to be accompanied. And not everyone wants to be accompanied by you. Some people will be wary of letting you in because other leaders have failed them, or because they do not trust you yet. Remember that oppression trauma is real. We cannot force people to be accompanied. It's up to them. Recognize also that people who have a more transactional view of leadership may think accompaniment is unnecessary or even a sign of "soft" (vs. strong) leadership. I learned this lesson after beginning a team meeting with a reflection, which was a typical practice at our university. I selected a beautiful children's picture book that was based on Leo Tolstoy's fable about life's purpose (Muth, 2002), because the theme was relevant given the low morale on campus. Although it resonated with several people, I later received a complaint that it was a waste of time. Even when we explain why we do what we do, not everyone will appreciate or want our *acompañamiento*.

It is challenging to know whether our efforts at accompaniment are successful without direct and indirect feedback. As you learn to accompany others, you can signal your openness to candid feedback: "I am new to this kind of listening but I want you to know that I truly want to hear what you have to say. If I do anything during this conversation that is invalidating or unhelpful, please let me know so I can do better." If someone shares that your attempts at *acompañamiento* have harmed them, listen nondefensively, believe them, apologize, and correct your behavior. To have the capacity to walk with others, we need to humbly accept that we are on a journey, especially as we learn how we have benefited from systems of oppression that have harmed our colleagues. This humility includes growing our critical awareness of internalized oppressive beliefs about our own marginalized identities. For instance, Lillian Comas-Díaz (2022) describes "colonial mentality" as internalized shame and inferiority among people who have experienced colonization. If a leader is unaware of their own colonial mentality, they may reinforce oppressive beliefs when they try to accompany others who share their identity.

Self-compassion is essential during this process, or we may not be ready to have compassion for those we accompany. We will make mistakes. The important thing is that we are trying to do better to change systems with and for others. People notice when you keep showing up.

Seek Out *Acompañamiento* for Yourself

Liberation work is relational and requires community. As Freire ([1970] 2000) notes, liberation involves dialogue founded, in part, on love for self and humanity. Yet I know many leaders who extend *acompañamiento* but are resistant to accepting it from others. Why? Part of the problem stems from the trope that successful leaders are above the fray; nothing affects us. We have also been socialized to believe that leaders must distance themselves from the people they lead. But serving as a leader with integrity does not mean that you need to hide who you are as a person. As people who are working toward a liberated future, we must acknowledge that leaders are not immune to the effects of stress and oppression. This is especially true for women and gender expansive people of the global majority and leaders with multiple marginalizations. There have been times when accompanying others reminded me of the harms I experienced and bore witness to. I have come to recognize that I need accompaniment to sustain my commitment and energy. Accompanying others without being accompanied is a recipe for bitterness, disengagement, and burnout. Try to welcome *acompañamiento* from loved ones, colleagues, and even direct reports, though they may not be able to know all the details of the situation because of ethical or legal considerations.

If you would like to offer accompaniment to others with more positional power and are not sure where to start, consider a short email or note acknowledging that you notice and are grateful for their efforts to create a healthier culture. Words of support, and an offer to contribute to the work if you have the bandwidth for it, may be just the *acompañamiento* the leader needs to keep going. When I stepped away from one of my leadership positions, I received several messages of solidarity from faculty and staff that signaled they appreciated me not just as an inclusive leader but as a human being. These messages were a strong witness to my experience.

For leaders who want to be accompanied, do not wait for others to recognize when you need it. Seek it out. I am constantly relearning to ask for and rely on the support and encouragement of like-minded people who share my values and understand where I am coming from. Know your limits, however. Sometimes people want to accompany you because it makes them feel better. If it makes you feel worse, find a way to disengage from the interaction or the relationship to protect your peace. Accompaniment can also come from spiritual sources and practices and the ancestors who have gone before us. I sometimes have conversations with my mother, who is deceased, about new opportunities and challenges that come my way. As she was someone who understood me and loved me unconditionally, I feel comforted by her presence. Seeking accompaniment for ourselves provides the nourishment we need to accompany others.

Summary

Acompañamiento consists of a set of practices that support liberation in our environments. With practice, liberatory leaders can create a foundation for accompaniment by building their empathic capacity and modeling psychological safety. They can build skills in empathic listening, responding, and action to cocreate systemic change in the face of oppression and nurture an appreciative culture. Yet *acompañamiento* is not a one-way street. Allowing ourselves to be on the receiving end of accompaniment builds up our fortitude, which is especially needed to engage in courageous action.

Questions for Reflection and Action

- How have others extended *acompañamiento* to you in the past? How did this accompaniment contribute to your own liberation and liberation in the workplace?
- How have you fallen into the trap of accompanying others from a place of superiority? How can you help colleagues who fall into this trap now?
- What has helped you build your empathic capacity? What can you do next to continue building this capacity?
- Identify a situation in which you were not able to listen mindfully to another at work. What interfered with your ability to tune in? If you had to replay the situation, what would you do differently?
- When was the last time you felt validated by someone else? What did they say or do to convey that they believed your experience?
- Describe a situation in which you have observed or directly experienced systemic action as the result of empathic listening.
- What steps can you take to seek the *acompañamiento* you need or desire?

CHAPTER 5

Leading Courageously When It Matters Most

Shortly after the January 6, 2021, insurrection at the US Capitol, I emailed faculty, staff, and students in my charge to acknowledge that I was distressed by the symbols of white supremacy and white Christian nationalism displayed by the people involved. I acknowledged that others may also have been upset by the events of the day. In my email, I explained that these feelings are a nudge for each of us to take a closer look at how we are complicit with oppressive systems. To support faculty and staff who wanted to take action, I offered to purchase one of two books for their personal work to combat oppression: Layla Saad's *Me and White Supremacy* (2020) or the edited volume *Presumed Incompetent II* (Flores Niemann, Gutiérrez y Muhs, and Gonzalez, 2020). Most of the responses I received were positive, with several recipients expressing gratitude that someone in leadership noticed the impact of this event on employees. Others went further and said that my email gave them the permission they didn't realize they needed to talk about difficult matters in their classrooms. And still others were motivated by the invitation to deepen their learning and recommit to justice in our work together. It was just an email and yet I was nervous about sending it. It was a risky move. I was in the first year of a new job at a new institution (an outsider!), the first Latine dean of this unit, and only the second woman. In the end, I decided it was the right thing to do because my action was aligned with my values and in service of others.

When does leading courageously matter most? From a liberation psychology perspective, courage matters most when the leader believes they have the most power to lose. Yet even small acts of courage produce meaningful ripple effects that lead to change. Leaders working toward liberation commit to engaging in acts of courage, no matter how small, to dismantle oppressive systems. Because many people are invested in maintaining the status quo (leaders included), this work necessarily risks our own comfort and power and sometimes our jobs. We can build our courage to take the actions required of us by recalling our mission and the power of liberatory leadership even in the midst of fear.

Before we delve into the ways in which courage manifests itself in our actions, let's acknowledge that the relative risk of any particular action is not the same for everyone. People who are subjected to multiple systems of oppression face greater personal and professional consequences when they act courageously than those with greater power and privilege. For instance, a straight white male leader may receive admiration from others for launching and leading an institutional strategic plan that advances justice and diversity, equity, and inclusion (DEI). A queer Black woman in the same position will likely face greater resistance because gendered racism and heteropatriarchal norms have taught others to minimize the importance of her work (e.g., "DEI is personal to her") or undervalue her competence. I once received anonymous feedback on a survey of my leadership that stated that I was "obsessed with DEI" and "meddlesome" in my work to advance faculty diversity and inclusion. One respondent went so far as to say I was an "unmitigated disaster" that should be stopped because of my attempts to infuse DEI into all aspects of our work. These comments were attempts to diminish equity work in general and to put me in my place. The risks and rewards of courageous action vary depending on who we are, who our colleagues are, our institutional and situational roles, our longevity with our organizations, and the setting, including geographic location. Each of us needs to evaluate the risks we are willing to take in a given situation and act accordingly. There is no one right way when it comes to courageous action.

For leaders engaged in liberation work, courage stems from critical self-awareness, an accurate reading of the reality, and *acompañamiento* so that we are prepared to engage in intentional and mission-focused action.

Courageous Actions Aligned with Liberatory Leadership

Liberating action centers the experiences of those who have been most harmed by oppressive systems. This action is the result of compassion and solidarity. And it requires coming face-to-face with our fears of the consequences. Think about times you have refrained from acting because you were afraid of what might happen next. Perhaps these questions passed through your mind: "Will my supervisors back me up, dismiss my concerns, or silence me? How will others respond? What if this action makes it difficult for me to do other things here that are important to me? What if I don't do it 'the right way'? What if people don't like me?" Full disclosure: these are questions that have often stalled me. I know I am not alone because I have worked with many academic leaders who held back because they were trapped by what-ifs. The moment to act then passed and they missed an opportunity to lead in a new way. As Ariana González Stokas (2023, 204) writes, "We who can afford the risks rarely take them and far too frequently place the interest of the institution (protection of the trustees, the president, or wealthy or vocal alums) above the work of justice. How reparation is unleashed is linked to the control and use of space and its liberative potential." When we act courageously, it can be a powerful, liberating force for ourselves and for others.

There are countless iterations of courageous action that are required of those who practice liberatory leadership. Nevertheless, leaders have the opportunity and the privilege to engage in several types of action that are especially needed to liberate academic cultures.

Courage to Address Institutional Wrongs

According to Jennifer Freyd, founder and CEO of the Center for Institutional Courage, and her colleague Carly Smith, institutions such as schools, churches, health-care organizations, and governments can betray the safety and well-being of people who depend on them (Smith and Freyd, 2013, 2014). Examples of institutional betrayal include leaders permitting credible sex offenders to continue to work at the institution and blaming targets of sexual harassment for their harassers' behaviors. Freyd and others have shown that institutional betrayal exacerbates the effects of trauma and harms all involved. Particularly damaging are institutional leaders' responses to wrongs that deny (D) the experience, attack the victim (A), and (R) reverse the victim (V) and offender (O) roles (DARVO; Freyd, n.d.).

The silence of leaders in response to reports of *academic* harassment can also constitute institutional betrayal. In cases of academic harassment and bullying, those with greater power and authority (e.g., tenured full professors) intimidate or attempt to control the actions of those with less power (e.g., untenured faculty, staff). According to communication scholar Loraleigh Keashly, academic harassment and bullying go unchecked because principles such as academic freedom and shared governance offer cover for bad behavior (Keashly, 2019). People who engage in academic harassment and bullying are excused for their behavior because they have "strong convictions," are "passionate" about their disciplines, or have personality quirks (e.g., "Don't take it personally; she's difficult because she's brilliant"). When people try to report this behavior, they are often silenced. For instance, an untenured colleague of mine once reported a pattern of academic harassment by a tenured colleague to a leader they believed could address the problem. But the leader minimized the concern and suggested that making a formal claim would reflect poorly on the reporter. Not surprisingly, the early career colleague did not pursue the claim further. The leader engaged in DARVO by stating that the victimized person's reputation would be attacked. We can speculate that an absence of policy for handling academic harassment may have been one reason for this betrayal. Or the leader may have felt personal discomfort or fear about the personal risks involved in holding others accountable, especially if the offender had powerful allies. Institutional cowardice—putting institutional risk management ahead of courageous action (Brown, 2021)—may be yet another reason for the betrayal. Whatever the reason, the leader put the institution's reputation and themselves before the needs of the more vulnerable person.

When these power dynamics are layered on top of white supremacist academic culture, harassment and bullying become even more problematic for people with marginalized identities. Think about the many times we have witnessed brilliant and talented colleagues of color DARVOed and pushed out of their departments or institutions because they spoke up for themselves, their students, or their colleagues in the face of academic harassment or maltreatment. They are blamed for not being respectful or collegial enough, not being grateful enough, or doing work that is not serious or important enough (e.g., epistemic exclusion; see Settles et al., 2021). Institutional betrayal of this sort not only harms the victimized person but also reinforces unjust and harmful narratives that are resistant to change.

There is an alternative. Leaders can engage in liberatory action and choose institutional courage. According to Freyd (2018), institutional courage reflects the organization's commitment to protect the people in its care. Institutional courage includes seeking the truth and engaging in just action even when it is unpleasant, is risky, and has short-term reputational and financial costs. Anyone who is acting as an institutional representative can respond with institutional courage. One of the bravest institutional responses I witnessed was by a department chair in response to a classroom invasion by a local community member who yelled sexist and racist slurs at the instructor of color and their students. Several university representatives minimized the immediate threat to the faculty and students and did not initially hold the person accountable for their actions. University personnel attempted to repair the situation and improve transparency through a series of communications; however, several missteps resulted in greater mistrust. Then a department chair, who was not the faculty member's chair, stepped in. This leader engaged in an act of institutional courage when they reported to me as their dean that they would not teach in person in the same building if it remained unlocked. I later learned that an untenured faculty member in the department had made this recommendation to their chair. The chair acted in solidarity with the instructor who experienced the attack, their own faculty colleague, and students, as well as out of concern for their own and others' physical and psychological safety. This was an exceptional act of courage because of the enormous pressure to teach in person at the time. It took courage for them to take this stand given their own marginalized identities, but they used their positional power in service of others. As dean, I was grateful for their courage. I referred to their declaration to continue to advocate for safe teaching spaces. This action and others led to some institutional changes to protect the safety and autonomy of faculty of color that semester. Although it did not solve every problem, it set an example of how to lead with solidarity and courage.

Courage to Center the Most Marginalized

Practicing liberatory leadership requires leaders to consider their own and others' identities when they respond to institutional wrongs. This awareness is especially needed in cases of contrapower harassment (DeSouza, 2011), when students, staff, or faculty harass or intimidate those with greater positional power and authority. Leaders may find that contrapower harassment is trickier to respond to when harassers hold dominant identities and targets hold marginalized identities. Positional authority is not the only identity marker for leaders to consider when responding with courage.

For instance, it may seem a simple situation when leaders must respond to a teacher's claim that their student is repeatedly emailing them for a better grade. A leader may counsel the instructor to hold firm and accept that this is what students do these days. But what if the student is threatening to show up at the instructor's home, or wealthy parents begin demanding a grade change? And what if the instructor is a Black woman and the student is a white man? Simply paying attention to who has the power to grant a grade is not enough. Leaders must center the experience of those with the least amount of power and agency in the sociopolitical context in which we live. Calling this out will likely violate the racist expectation that white people are the primary beneficiaries of the privileges associated with higher education, an assumption that Victor Ray describes in his "Theory of Racialized Organizations" (2019). Leaders must have the courage to address anger from contrapower harassers and their allies. Such harassers feel entitled to a benefit that has not been granted by people with marginalized identities, who they assume lack the competence to be leaders. Standing in solidarity with the target takes strength and time because the leader must do their homework to get the facts and assess all of the power dynamics at play.

The target's and the harasser's identities are not the only factors, however. Leaders must also be aware of the ways in which their own privileged and marginalized identities may reinforce oppression or create openings for growth and liberation. Take the contrapower harassment situation of the white male student and his parents demanding that the Black woman faculty member change his grade. Now imagine that it involves a Black male department chair minimizing the experience of the instructor and encouraging her to change the grade even after hearing her out about the student's missed assignments. In this case, institutional betrayal is compounded by cultural betrayal because the leader and target share the same marginalized identity, a concept Tayler Mathews (2017) calls institutional cultural betrayal. Jennifer M. Gómez (2023a) developed cultural betrayal trauma theory to describe what happens when (intra) cultural trust and solidarity are betrayed by members of one's own marginalized group. According to Gómez, who studies abuse by Black men against Black women and girls, (intra)cultural trust and solidarity are strategies to survive and thrive in the context of racism. Abuse and violence by a Black man toward a Black woman violates this trust. Whether she reports the abuse or not, she experiences harm; she either risks reporting about someone from her own cultural group who reinforces racist and sexualized stereotypes of Black men, or she remains silent and does not receive justice and healing. Applying this concept to institutional betrayal, the presumed safety offered by a leader of color is stripped away. In addition, there may be (intra)cultural pressure to remain silent so as not to reinforce racist stereotypes about the leadership competencies of people of color. This experience can be particularly demoralizing at predominantly white institutions, where faculty of the global majority are already isolated and are chronically made to feel they do not belong. In addition, the target will likely experience more isolation and injustice. Applying Eduardo Bonilla-Silva's (2017) concept of "false positives," leaders with marginalized identities who internalize harmful beliefs can become harassers who perpetrate cultural betrayal toward people with whom they share identities. They are false positives because these leaders were thought to bring greater diversity and equity but they are actually working against it. These leaders may also gain privileges from proximity to whiteness and power that protect them from reprimands.

Yet it doesn't have to be this way. Leaders who engage in critical consciousness to understand how they show up and consider the complexity of the situations they face will be more open to recognizing the power dynamics that need to shift. Leaders can learn a lot about what types of courageous action are needed if they practice *acompañamiento* and listen with humility and curiosity, without centering themselves as a savior. As leaders, we must increase our awareness of who in our charge might be more vulnerable to attack by others who hold power derived from institutional longevity, positional power, or the power that comes with privileged identities. We can ask the people in our charge what they would like from us. Leaders can also stand with their peers and those with greater authority, especially those with marginalized identities, who are fostering courageous change throughout the system. Again, we must ask how we can help, and then support their work publicly and privately and contribute to it in tangible ways, including through time and funds. Crucially, leaders must hold people accountable when they engage in harmful behaviors that maintain oppressive cultures.

Courage to Hold People Accountable

It can take courage to hold people accountable for their actions, especially in oppressive academic environments in which accountability is not the norm. I have witnessed the fear and trepidation up and down the hierarchy when leaders must provide feedback and share expectations for change with another person.

I have felt it myself. It is a little surprising given that faculty and staff seem to feel very comfortable holding students accountable. Unfortunately, most of us were never trained to do the same with our colleagues. Notions of academic freedom and autonomy reinforce a hands-off "live and let live" mentality. When these beliefs occur at institutions that pride themselves on their "culture of nice," it becomes even more difficult to have accountability conversations. Linda Hartling and Elizabeth Sparks (2010) refer to these cultures as "pseudo-relational cultures" because authentic conversations in which people might become uncomfortable are avoided. We need to dispense with the oppressive idea that academics are free to behave any way they choose, without regard for others. We also must recognize that excusing oneself from the responsibility to hold others accountable can perpetuate oppression. Inaction is a choice, and one often stemming from privilege.

Liberatory leadership calls us to tell people when they have caused harm even when such harm was not intended. The alternative is to allow people to continue to engage in behaviors that oppress others. Inaction is also harmful to the person engaging in the behavior, as others may begin to avoid them; the offender can become alienated or bitter and perpetuate unhealthy environments for others. The compassionate thing to do when someone is behaving badly is to give them honest feedback and an opportunity to change course.

As leaders, we must also be compassionate with ourselves as we discover why giving this kind of feedback makes us uncomfortable. It might be that we have discomfort because we lack training and practice. It may also be that we are fearful of the consequences of accountability for ourselves: "I'm not as kind as I thought I was because I'm giving this feedback," "If I tell this person they are engaging in bullying behavior, they'll be mad at me," "This person is very powerful and I might make some enemies," or, "I will make a mistake and make things even worse." Critical consciousness requires us to take a good look at the narratives that block our work as liberatory leaders.

Even though it might be frightening to give honest feedback, it is wonderful when people take it to heart. In one case, I shared feedback from students of color to a faculty member about his microaggressive behaviors. With humility, he asked for guidance and we had a fruitful discussion about corrective next steps. It is also true, because of the lack of accountability inherent in academia, that you may be the first person to ever provide this feedback. If that is the case, it is wise to be prepared for an initial response characterized by defensiveness and anger: "No one has ever told me this before, so I don't believe it's a problem!" I once had a string of accountability conversations with men whose students reported gender-based microaggressions in the classroom. In each case, the instructor DARVOed the students. They denied they did anything wrong, blamed the students for their misinterpretations, became the victimized person in their own eyes, or reported (paternalistically) that they were just looking out for the students when they commented on their appearance or behavior. This was the first time each of them was being held accountable for their behaviors. This is where compassion comes in. I told them I knew it was difficult to receive this information because no one ever gave them this feedback before. I shared that it was important for us to talk about it because I knew they cared about students and the quality of the classroom environment. I wanted them to know how their behaviors were being received so they could adjust and continue to contribute to our learning community. I treated them as human beings worthy of dignity and honesty. Truthfully, these were not pleasant conversations and not all of the instructors appreciated the discussion in the moment. But I learned some things about the norms in their discipline and culture, their expectations of the faculty-student relationship, and their concerns. Because I was plain with them, they had concrete action steps to create psychologically safer classrooms. Recall that an assumption of leading toward liberation is that everyone is harmed from oppressive systems. This means that leaders must accompany everyone with compassion, including those who make mistakes.

These conversations can be trickier for leaders with marginalized identities who address behaviors in those with more privileged identities. My authority as a dean may be questioned more by someone who is angry at being held accountable by a Latine person and a woman. I have also witnessed those with a mix of privileged and marginalized identities resist accountability by focusing on their marginalizations. A white male tenured faculty member with a marginalized identity once reported to institutional authorities that I created a psychologically unsafe environment for him because I had invited him to a one-on-one meeting to talk about his threatening behavior during an invited talk he attended. Several faculty had witnessed him accusing the speaker, a person of the global majority, of bias and discrimination in their research talk. It was my job to learn why he behaved the way he did, provide feedback on how his words were received, and discuss more productive ways of expressing his concerns in the future. His reaction to my invitation (i.e., to report me) was telling. He was not accustomed to accounting for his behavior, and he was not aware of how his own behaviors contributed to a feeling of unsafety, not just for his peers but also for untenured colleagues who were worried about how we would behave should he serve on their tenure and promotion committees. Instead, he focused on his marginalized identity and did not recognize the power he had as a white male tenured professor. Situations like this one require leaders to learn how to hold themselves accountable and manage competing perceptions of vulnerability and authoritarian power.

Liberatory leaders can hold peers and colleagues accountable for their behaviors even if we have no formal authority over them. Most institutions have policies for sexual harassment and bias reporting, which notifies those with the authority to investigate further, but there are many harmful behaviors that fall outside reporting requirements. Still, there may be offices or trusted leaders who can provide coaching or offer assistance in other ways. In the prior example, people who witnessed the behavior came to me because they trusted me and also did not feel safe having the conversation with their colleague. They trusted me because I consistently communicated that I wanted to hear the good, the bad, and the ugly about our culture. Be the leader who signals this trust. If we don't know what's going on, we cannot do anything about it.

There will be instances when you can hold your colleagues accountable, even if it feels difficult. I once observed a senior white woman faculty member repeatedly cut off a Black woman faculty member in a meeting I led. It didn't sit well with me, but I was not sure if my early-career colleague shared that experience. I checked in with her afterward, and she acknowledged that she was hesitant to attend future meetings because she felt silenced and devalued. She gave me permission to share my own observations about the senior colleague's behavior from my perspective as chair of the committee. We agreed that making it about my concerns protected her from having to do so as the less powerful person in the situation. I went into that meeting with some fear about getting my senior colleague angry and with a feeling of awkwardness from not having much practice with this kind of conversation. The senior colleague was surprised but reflective and offered that her own experience of being devalued as a scholar may have contributed to her wanting to "own" the discussion. Our conversation bore some fruit. She reported a stronger motivation to consider the impact of actions on others, especially women of color. There was greater trust between us because I was honest about what I observed. What about the experience of the early-career faculty member? Unfortunately, she reported that she continued to experience invalidation from the senior colleague in other situations. One could argue that accountability failed. Why would we gather up the courage to do this work if it did not permanently change the senior colleague's behavior? Importantly, the early-career colleague reported that my witness and our collaboration on how to address the problem validated her experience in a meaningful way. She knew she had an ally who was willing to work with and for her. I also learned some valuable lessons, including that sustainable team effort is necessary to change culture. While we might want a single conversation to solve all our problems, we should recognize that accountability must be sustained over time and owned by more than one person to effect lasting, liberatory change.

It is difficult when the person to be held accountable appears to wield their power in purposefully abusive ways. Even in these cases, compassion is required. I have been able to build greater compassion in these instances when I take the time to learn more about the person. Almost always, oppressive systems or practices have harmed them too. Compassion gives me the courage to hold them accountable and the confidence to do it in a way that honors their dignity as a human being. If you are the leader who must address the behavior directly, it is wise to receive counsel from other courageous leaders and match your response to the situation. In some cases, a discussion with informal follow-up is all that is required. In others, a letter to a personnel file, a formal report or investigation, or other consequences are required in line with institutional policies and federal and state laws. These courageous actions contribute to culture change as others observe that they are taken seriously and can depend on accountability.

Courage to Be Open to Liberating Change

Leading culture change is courageous because higher education is rooted in white supremacist and patriarchal culture. Any change that moves away from these cultural norms, including attempts to change policies, practices, and procedures, or even simply question them, will be met with resistance such as, "We've tried that before and it didn't work," or the paternalistic "Let me do you a favor and tell you how we do that here." Cultural courage can begin with questions and curiosity: Why do we do it that way? Who benefits from us doing this a particular way? Who decided we should do it this way? Asking questions is one way to begin to scan the environment, assess readiness for liberating change, and strategize a way forward. Curiosity also shows others who share our questions that we invite their ideas and observations, further opening the possibility of change through shared leadership. How people respond to these questions, with mutual curiosity or paternalizing responses, reveals like-minded allies and obstacles to change.

Efforts to improve transparency can also be courageous because status quo cultures often restrict the flow of information or access to resources to a privileged few. For instance, at one of my universities, only some faculty knew they could ask for additional funding to accompany their students to conferences. This policy was not written anywhere. The people who were not "in the know" were often early-career colleagues with lower salaries, colleagues from smaller departments, or those with smaller networks. They ended up paying out of pocket or not accompanying their students at all, while others who were aware of the policy were able to supplement their travel funding to be with their students. We corrected this disparity by adding language in our policy and disseminating this information widely. Another way to foster culture change is to create and share selection rubrics for awards and recognition. Rubrics must be created with input from the people who apply as well as those who evaluate the materials. Periodic rubric review and the use of equity advocates ensure processes remain as free from bias as possible. These and other helpful strategies to increase transparency and equity can be found on the website of the ADVANCE Resource and Coordination Network for STEM equity and in the books *An Inclusive Academy: Achieving Diversity and Excellence* (Stewart and Valian, 2018) and *Doing the Right Thing: How Colleges and Universities Can Undo Systemic Racism in Faculty Hiring* (Gasman, 2022).

Greater transparency can also be brought to how groups work together. For instance, faculty and student affairs staff often create community agreements that describe guidelines for respectful and inclusive classes and student meetings. It is then surprising to see how infrequently faculty and staff apply the same principles to making group norms more apparent when working together. Think of the many times in committee meetings when someone speaks over a colleague, rolls their eyes so everyone can see, or derails the conversation. Often, the default reaction is for people to look down or share a snide expression with a peer who is observing the same thing. Worse, an argument may break out or someone may leave the room. Developing community agreements is one way to get everyone on the same page to identify shared norms and a process for getting back on track when a colleague violates the agreement. Bylaws take this work one step further by articulating how decisions get made and by whom.

Changes like these might not seem courageous at first glance. But don't confuse important procedural work with administrative drudgery! In fact, because status quo cultures oppress through the presence and absence of policies, expect resistance. That's why courage is required. I discovered this when I asked all of the department chairs in my unit to develop community agreements and bylaws in collaboration with their faculty and staff. One department chair told me that they did not want to even "go there" with community agreements because she feared that historical tensions in the department would erupt into outright war. Another chair told me that some tenured faculty in their unit argued to exclude non-tenure-track faculty when framing community agreements and bylaws. Leaders will need to stay the course and address the fears that may surface in response to this kind of change. Fears include loss of tangible or intangible privileges like who gets the best office or teaching schedule, or whose opinion matters. But culture change is not a zero-sum game with winners and losers. If everyone is indeed harmed by oppressive practices, then the leader must also share how holding on to some of these perceived privileges harms everyone, including the students we serve. To persist in this work, leaders can recall their reason for practicing liberatory leadership. In addition, when enacting change, it is essential to find your allies and build up other leaders. Remember that liberation is about what we cocreate with others.

More on the Consequences of Courageous Action

Recall my email about the insurrection in the nation's capital on January 6, 2021. I received three responses from people who disagreed with me: two from students and one from a faculty member. The students claimed my message was antiwhite and anti-Christian because I mentioned white supremacy and white Christian nationalism. One of them demanded a public apology. This kind of reaction should not be a surprise to leaders working toward liberation because calling out, let alone dismantling, systems of power results in attempts to discredit or undermine us.

These responses also illustrate that courageous action is not "one and done"; courage is a commitment and requires sustained action. I could have ignored the students. Instead, I invited the students to speak with me (the faculty member did not request a meeting or ask me to apologize). I recognized I had an opportunity to engage these students on behalf of others who might not have the same opportunity (e.g., their peers in the classroom, instructors and staff of color, and others who experienced the insurrection as harmful). Early in the conversation, it was clear to me that these students were not aware of white Christian nationalism as a movement in the United States. They did not understand that white supremacy is an ideology that could be espoused by anyone, Black and Brown people included. At that point, I acknowledged we were not going to agree about the meaning of the events and I invited them to engage in additional conversations with me in the future. One of the students appeared interested, and the other rolled their eyes at me. I realized these first-year college students were about to be exposed to their peers' diversity of lived experiences and to an education that included the history of social, political, and religious movements. Yet it took some emotional and spiritual wherewithal for me to engage these students calmly in the moment. It helped that my supervisors supported my efforts, but I still needed some time to process this conversation in light of current events and my place in the world. Compassion and courage require energy.

The entire experience, while stressful at times, gave me hope. I learned something about the impact of my public actions and about my new institution. I raised awareness and empowered others to engage in the work of liberation. I found new allies.

Summary

Each of us must assess our comfort level and relative risk given our positions and identities, yet everyone can practice courage in their own ways. We can show courage by taking responsibility for our actions, centering the most marginalized and excluded, holding others accountable, and remaining open to liberating change we might not have imagined yet. All of this requires humility and a willingness to risk offending others who have benefited and continue to benefit from oppression. Courageous action also requires that we accept feeling afraid at times. As psychotherapist Judith Jordan (2010, 32) writes, "Courage involves feeling the fear and finding support to deal with it." The rewards are great when we consider that we are preparing the ground for those who come after us. As noted academic leader and plant biologist Beronda Montgomery (2021, 93) writes, the effort of disruptive leaders "leads to additional ecosystem changes that support the next wave of individuals needed to drive and sustain cultural change and institutional transformation." Courageous action seeds change. Some of this change is embodied in the people we "en-courage" through liberatory leadership development opportunities.

Questions for Reflection and Action

- Think about an institutionally courageous response you have witnessed or experienced. How might this example inspire you to lead more courageously?
- If you have multiple marginalized identities, whom in your community of support can you call on to help build your courage? How can you, in turn, build their community of support? How can you communicate your needs to better pursue liberatory leadership practices?
- If you have predominantly privileged identities (e.g., in a position of authority, wealthy, white, male, and straight), what can you do to be a more effective ally to others at your institution? Include steps for colleagues with less power, such as your direct reports; peers; and those with greater power and authority, such as those you report to. How can you ensure you are not falling into the savior or hero trap when acting with courage?

- Most of us have a blend of marginalized and privileged identities. In what ways can you use your privilege to accompany and support others who do not share those privileges?
- What do you need from your community of support to strengthen your courage? For instance, do you need to talk out your plan, practice what you will say or write, or have a safe person challenge you so you are prepared to respond to pushback?
- Fear can be an obstacle to courageous action. Here are several questions aimed at freeing you from fear so you are free to act courageously:
  - How might reconnecting with your values strengthen your resolve to act courageously?
  - What frightens you most when you consider a courageous action you have planned (e.g., attachment to being liked, threats to your reputation, threats to your job or financial safety, loss of power, other fears)?
  - Who are the most powerless or disenfranchised, and how would they benefit from your courageous action? How might you benefit?
  - Even if your planned action "fails," what seeds might you be planting with this courageous action?

CHAPTER 6

Growing Liberatory Leadership Skills in Others

As a new associate provost charged with faculty and academic staff development, one of my first tasks was to develop and launch a new leadership academy. The provost was a Black man who appreciated the need for broadened and inclusive access to mentoring and professional development. He recognized that there were many talented people who were excluded from leadership pipelines. He also knew that greater inclusion and skills building in faculty and staff could improve the student learning environment. When we launched the faculty-staff leadership academy, most of the applicants were women across races and people of the global majority. These were outstanding colleagues with innovative ideas, many generated from their own lived experiences of exclusion or from working in solidarity with those who had experienced marginalization. Before this experience, their talents were often invisible to leaders and they had had limited opportunities for leadership growth. The program was intentionally designed to elevate their leadership and improve quality of life across the institution. Through skills-based workshops, mentorship and sponsorship, and cohort building, the program led to new initiatives for which participants served as leaders. The yearlong academy healed some of the harm resulting from isolation, feelings of imposterism, and hopelessness imposed by oppressive academic culture and a history of exclusion at this institution.

Growing leadership skills in others is a liberatory act. When we invest in others, they feel valued and empowered to act on their vision and creativity to make life better for themselves, their colleagues, and their students. As a community of learners, we can cocreate environments in which everyone can contribute to change together.

One might argue that a focus on developing individual leaders is antithetical to the work of collective liberation and solidarity. After all, many of us are familiar with oppressive leaders who handpick their successors or lavish attention on people who cozy up to them. Perhaps they only send their "favorites" to leadership development programs. To be sure, traditional leadership development can reinforce hierarchical power structures in higher education. Author and activist Paulo Freire ([1970] 2000) admits that whereas there is a time and place for leaders to direct and coordinate the work of others, the problem lies in leaders who believe they are depositing their singular wisdom into their mentees. These mentees will then lead exactly as they have led.

Our job is not to create a "mini-me" who mimics us. Rather, liberatory leaders embrace growing leadership skills in others as a humanizing process of liberation in which leader and mentee learn from each other and contribute to collective liberation. Envisioning many possible futures, liberatory leaders apply a decolonial approach to leadership development that honors mentees' own individuality, creativity, and knowledge. According to theologians Elizabeth Gandolfo and Laurel Potter (2022), who wrote about the Comunidades Eclesiales de Base (CEBs) and their relationships with institutional leaders, this decolonial praxis requires us to be known, to be re-created, and to engage in sustained and collective action with others. Leaders work with and for others so that future leaders have the capacity to engage in self-reflection, read historical and contemporary realities, accompany others, and courageously solve problems in collaboration with others. The system cannot change without a critical mass of liberatory leaders working together to cocreate new ways of doing things.

In this chapter, I provide concrete ideas to grow liberatory leadership skills in others. One strategy is to create a leadership development program; however, there are many other ways to build leadership skills, including intentionally and transparently sharing information, serving as a mentor or sponsor to emerging leaders, and encouraging grassroots leadership efforts through emergent change leadership principles. Each of these strategies, independently and as a multipronged approach, can be used to cocreate a liberating future with others.

Reveal the Hidden Curriculum

Leaders can support a more inclusive vision of leadership by revealing the hidden curriculum—the norms, practices, and knowledge that are available to the few with the right connections or prior knowledge and experience. Revealing the hidden curriculum is often a goal for those who have experienced exclusion of one form or another. This is the case for me, a first-generation college graduate who learned early on that my peers had access to information that I did not have, including how to study and how to write papers, not to mention how to navigate affluent social culture. I had to learn skills on my own through trial and error or by asking a lot of pointed questions. It was exhausting, and for a while I wondered if I belonged. The best instructors made plain what they were asking and did not assume that all their students had the same preparation. They did not make success dependent on guessing what the instructor wanted. Perhaps you can identify with this situation as an educator, as a student, or both. We can translate these experiences to leadership.

For instance, negotiating a tenure-track faculty job can be a mystery. I remember what it was like as a new faculty member, not knowing how negotiation worked and feeling quite powerless in the situation. There were times when it seemed like a dean or department chair and I were competing, rather than collaborating, in the negotiation process. When I became a hiring manager and negotiated with faculty candidates, I took a different tack. I explained how negotiation worked with me. I told candidates that they should ask for what they needed in a startup package because I wanted them to be successful and happy. I also told them that I would not rescind an offer if they asked for too much. The worst that could happen was that I would tell them I couldn't meet their request. If I was not able to provide what they requested, I would be up front about what I could offer and why. I knew this approach was unusual because most candidates expressed surprise and relief. As a leader practicing liberation, I wanted people to have all the information they needed to make a decision that was good for them and the organization they were entering. It is possible to reveal the hidden curriculum in many other situations, including by explaining budget decisions and policy exceptions. Put yourself in the shoes of your people and consider what information they may not have because of lack of experience, mentoring, or insider knowledge through their networks. Trust that they also have the knowledge and experience that you do not have to make wise choices. Freeing up the system means freely sharing knowledge and information, including your read of reality, so that everyone is empowered to make good decisions.

The hidden curriculum can also be uncovered by harnessing the collective wisdom of the community. On some level, people are aware of the power of community, but they are often held back by academic siloes, hierarchical organizational structure, and fear. The siloing of academia, for instance, often leads faculty and staff to engage in a merely transactional way that prevents them from learning from each other. Within disciplines, faculty may gravitate toward colleagues studying similar topics rather than considering how others outside their discipline might contribute to new, creative solutions. Hierarchical organizational norms also constrict spheres of interaction across the organizational chart. People with less power in the institution are made to feel like it's not their place to get to know someone with more power, and people with more power are made to feel like they must spend their limited time with other leaders at their level or above. Finally, it can be anxiety provoking to reach out to others we don't know without an explicit problem to solve. Inviting someone to meet just to get to know them is antithetical to white supremacy cultural norms that focus on productivity and time urgency. Yet leaders can seed change with those meetings by bridging across lived experiences, finding common ground, developing a common read of the institutional context, and spreading knowledge.

Liberatory leaders can recognize and resist these barriers to building community by encouraging networking. In addition to being available to others with less power through *acompaña-miento*, liberatory leaders can also openly talk about the value of networking for themselves and for others. Every time I have given a presentation about networking at the institutions I've worked at, people have reached out to me for coffee to learn more and build relationships. Simply talking about networking was a liberating experience that led to action. In addition, leaders can share tools for evaluating one's existing network so that others are able to meet new colleagues with intentionality. Mapping one's network may help people recognize that they may benefit from increasing the diversity of their network to include people across ranks and titles, disciplines, and lived experiences.

Leaders can also make the needed introductions to foster community building. I have two colleagues, both women leaders of color, who use their knowledge and power to build other people's networks. What sets them apart from other leaders is that they do not wait to be asked to make these introductions. They also do not restrict these connection opportunities to those with similar disciplines, ranks, or titles. Instead, they each embrace their knowledge of and experience with oppression by spontaneously introducing people with similar values to build a liberating future. In their introductions, they highlight the strengths that each person could bring to the relationship. These colleagues seed additional liberation in the new connections they foster. As Linda Hartling and Elizabeth Sparks (2008, 2010) note, networking in the name of community building can transform culture. Networking can change how people relate to each other, solve problems together, and foster mutual growth and learning.

In addition to networking and building community, we can reveal the hidden curriculum by giving away our hard-earned wisdom. Share strategies and methods that have worked for you and how they represent your understanding of liberatory leadership. From how you craft an email to how you reach out to others for input, information about what works can be enlightening to others. It is just as important to share about difficulties and failures as it is about our successes. For instance, I have often shared my story about a particularly disappointing job interview that occurred early in my career. During my job talk at a prestigious university, I was interrupted constantly until a faculty member asked everyone to wait until the question-and-answer portion. After the talk, my host told me that the audience did not think I went about testing my hypotheses in the brightest manner. Ouch! I felt demoralized and like I was not cut out to be a professor. Later, I learned about the hypercompetitive and oppressive environment in that department. There are many lessons packed into this story, including the fact that candidates can claim their agency by making a statement about when questions are welcomed. Another lesson is that every department, unit, or institution has a culture that is difficult to hide; it is possible to read the environment for signs of healthy and unhealthy culture. And still another lesson is that people with power do not have the final say; they can be wrong about our potential. I went on to publish the work from my job talk in the top journal in my field. When I share this story with others as *testimonio*, I reveal the norms that were and still are at work in the academy so that others can resist similar situations with knowledge, confidence, and power.

Finally, invite your team to participate in problem-solving that traditionally only required your input. When it is ethically and legally responsible to do so, ask for their opinion and truly weigh their insights about difficult personnel or budget decisions. Explain what you are asking for from your team so they can provide better-quality information or help you understand why you might need different information from what you first requested. Explain to them why you are doing something a particular way or why a seemingly minor comment was more meaningful than it might have seemed at first glance. Be patient as your team learns that you value their ideas and leadership. In one of my teams, it was so unusual for a leader in my position to ask for input from others that it took a full year for people to trust that I was not simply paying lip service to "What do you think about this problem?" or "How should we go about fixing this inequity?"

In addition to treating others with less power and privilege as knowledgeable equals, modeling is critical to reveal the hidden curriculum. Allow people to learn by observing you in action. I once asked a colleague on my team to accompany me to a meeting about a department's culture and climate. I wanted my colleague to observe how I handled pushback about a decision I had made because I expected that he would be put in a similar situation in the future. I also wanted him to be prepared for overt and subtle resistance to change in this department. After the meeting, we were able to debrief and compare notes. It was insightful for my colleague to observe how I navigated the discussion. I also benefited from his valuable observations and advice, since he was able to pay attention to dynamics in ways I could not. Although I took the initiative to address an aspect of the hidden curriculum with my colleague, we both learned from the experience to support the work of liberation.

Mentorship and Sponsorship

Beronda Montgomery (2020a) observes that the typical academic leadership training journey is one of copying the status quo. Leaders are often trained on meeting institutional goals and maintaining systems of gatekeeping. In contrast to gatekeeping, Montgomery urges leaders to engage in "groundskeeping," tending to the ecosystem to support individuals' values-based goals even as they fulfill institutional goals. Applying a liberatory lens to the concept of groundskeeping means that leaders honor individuality in people's desired trajectories and engage in systems change to ensure that institutional goals are not harmful.

Mentorship is one way to groundskeep. Through mentoring, we honor and value the chosen life direction of another. Mentors provide emotional support, advice, feedback, and coaching to protégés. Sponsors go even further by advocating for others. Effective sponsors use their power, authority, and prestige to create opportunities for others with less power (Ibarra and Simmons, 2023). Rosalind Chow (2021) describes sponsorship as a form of influence in which the sponsor actively cultivates a positive impression of the protégé in front of other powerful people. Mentors can be sponsors, but Chow notes that some mentors cannot effectively serve as sponsors. They may not have the authority, power, or social capital to effectively "talk up" their protégés to others. Another obstacle to sponsorship is fear. Leaders might not feel comfortable taking the risk that sponsorship entails. For instance, it may reflect poorly on the leader if the protégé fails to meet expectations.

When sponsorship is done right, it is characterized by amplifying, boosting, connecting, and defending (Chow, 2021).

Amplification happens when leaders create a positive impression of the protégé by talking up the protégé's accomplishments and skills to powerful others. Boosting includes expressing confidence in the protégé's skills through nominations and recommendations. Connecting occurs when leaders make introductions or invite the protégé to meetings with powerful others. The most courageous sponsorship behavior is perhaps the most important for liberatory leaders: defending. Leaders who defend their protégés behind closed doors put their reputation on the line by offering an alternative explanation for others' negative reports or impressions. This is risky because, if attitudes are not changed, it could result in a loss of social capital for the leader. Leaders with multiple dominant identities, especially married cisgender straight white males, have less to lose given their de facto power in US higher education. Because of this security and privilege, Chow urges leaders with dominant identities to sponsor emerging and seasoned leaders with one or more marginalized identities to advance social equity. In addition to sponsorship, liberatory leaders engage in self-reflection to learn if there are oppressive patterns in their sponsorship behavior and make changes if necessary.

Beware of paternalism disguised as sponsorship. When I was advancing diversity, equity, and inclusion (DEI) at one institution, individuals (mostly white men) would complain periodically to senior leaders that I was too focused on DEI. They felt excluded by my efforts, which they also perceived as being antithetical to academic excellence. They could not understand or embrace the idea of inclusive excellence (D. Williams, Berger, and McClendon, 2005). The more skilled of these reporters would couch their complaints by stating, "Of course diversity is nice to have, but she is going too far," referring to my efforts to integrate

DEI into recruitment, hiring, and curriculum development. I expected senior leadership, which was composed mostly of white men, to defend me because I was hired to do this work. Instead, leaders gave ear to these critics, which only validated the complaints and made my efforts more difficult. They explained that validating the concerns of these people and bending to their critiques was a political necessity. They also gave me other advice about how to be "political" that I did not perceive to be helpful given my social location as a Latina woman advancing DEI. In their paternalism, they missed an opportunity to serve as a sponsor to me.

Sponsorship is critical for leaders with multiple marginalizations. For instance, in their original research on the pet-to-threat phenomenon, organizational psychologist and leader Kecia Thomas and her colleagues chronicled how Black women in subordinate positions are often perceived as "pets" when they join an organization (Thomas et al., 2013). They are championed and celebrated until they gain greater power and authority. Then they are perceived as threats that need to be managed. I have personally observed this trajectory among faculty and staff colleagues many times at different universities. It is also evident in a recent study of chief diversity officers (CDOs), most of whom were Black women respondents: "CDOs with less than one year of experience tended to report 'broad-based buy-in,' 'strong alignment' with 'other campus units' and having 'a meaningful seat at the table,' but such signs of support tended to be proportionately less prevalent the longer a respondent's tenure as CDO" (Swartout et al., 2023, 3). Effective mentors and sponsors are aware of and work to counteract oppressive shifts in power dynamics, especially when working with people who have experienced past and current marginalization and exclusion.

From a liberatory perspective, mentoring and sponsoring are not one-way streets; protégés are not the only beneficiaries of the relationship. Critical self-reflection and *acompañamiento* necessarily mean that liberatory leaders will also be transformed by mentoring and sponsoring others. I do not think I am alone when I say that I have learned a lot about what it means to practice liberation and courage from colleagues and students I have mentored and sponsored. In fact, they are the ones who inspired me to write this book.

Collective Leadership Development

Teaching the hidden curriculum and engaging in sponsorship are two ways leaders can help others develop their skills, but they are not sufficient from a liberatory perspective. Leaders must actively work against the temptation to train only the few they deem worthy. As Freire ([1970] 2000, 143) writes, "Oppressors do not favor promoting the community as a whole, but rather selected leaders. The latter course, by preserving a state of alienation, hinders the emergence of consciousness and critical intervention in a total reality." To disrupt the practice of individualizing leadership through selected paths for the few, liberatory leaders can seek out opportunities to grow the leadership capacity of the entire community. The CEBs of El Salvador developed a communal consciousness of oppression so that everyone could participate in the creative reimagining of how their collective action could lead to liberation (Gandolfo and Potter, 2022). Liberatory leaders can foster this collective movement toward leadership through methods of bringing people together to collaborate on projects, as well as formal and informal leadership development opportunities that emphasize learning and collaboration in community with others.

Emergent Change Leadership

With the knowledge you built during your environmental scan, consider new ways of bringing people together that encourage bridging faculty-staff or disciplinary divides. Populate teams and working groups with people who have diverse skills, life experiences, and knowledge. In addition, ensure that teams articulate clear rules for engagement about how the work gets done and how meetings are facilitated so that everyone feels safe to contribute. If needed, help the team read the reality of the situation or problem so that they can better identify systemic oppression and possible solutions. Above all, trust their experience. With these strategies, leadership is open to all, even without titles.

I stumbled onto this strategy as a new dean trying to advance DEI in the midst of the COVID-19 pandemic and the national reckoning with anti-Black racism. Through my expertise in integrating DEI into higher education initiatives at another institution, I knew that faculty and staff were experts of their own experiences at this institution. They probably had many ideas about how to cocreate a more inclusive learning and work environment. I was pleasantly surprised when 40 people signed up to be part of a grassroots DEI initiative. Through our meetings, the community identified several priorities, including faculty and staff recruitment and STEM education. Soon we invited students because they would be directly or indirectly affected by our work. Over time, the working groups adapted to fit changing needs. They accomplished several goals, including developing and practicing guidelines for equitable hiring and creating a learning community for equity-minded teaching. When the door was thrown open to create inclusive teams, people were able to lead culture change and learn from each other. It was inspiring to witness.

My role as a leader was not to dictate what was done but to set a liberatory direction with some parameters to help people carry out their projects. Organizational change expert Deborah Rowland (2017) calls this approach "emergent change." With emergent change, the leader sets the intention and direction, provides some guardrails, and then gets out of the way. In my example, the main intention was for the group to identify and work toward outcomes that resulted in a healthier workplace for everyone, especially those most marginalized and excluded. The guardrails included reminders about the scope of our work (some wanted to change other aspects of the university that were not within our control), flexible deadlines to work toward, and periodic check-ins with me so that I could offer support, answer questions, and connect the groups with others across campus who could help achieve our goals. I also asked coaching questions like, "How will this create a more equitable environment?" "Who else needs to be invited to this discussion?" "How do we measure success?" and, "What is reasonable in terms of project scope and timeline given the other demands on your time and energy?" My role was to listen with *acompañamiento* and recognize their wisdom so that they could lead change that mattered to them. This experience was one of the more satisfying accomplishments of my career because I served as an *animadora* (facilitator) of change and learned in the process. It also reenergized many of the participants who had been desiring change but had no clear path forward.

When you begin to do emergent change work, you may find that people initially struggle with the expansiveness of the possibilities. It may appear that they are not able to identify or develop solutions. Ariana González Stokas (2023) explains that a common result of epistemic oppression is an initial lack of creativity. When people have been questioned, silenced, or attacked for their ideas, they stop dreaming. So be patient as people develop psychological safety and reclaim their creativity and agency to solve problems.

Formal Leadership Development

Several organizations, university consortia, disciplinary societies, and companies offer leadership development programs for higher education faculty, staff, and administrators. Participating in these programs can help emerging and seasoned leaders identify their strengths, practice leadership skills, and network with professionals at other institutions. These programs can be costly, which often restricts participation to people who work at affluent institutions or who have leaders who know firsthand about the value of these programs. As a cost-effective alternative, some colleges and universities have begun to create in-house leadership development programs.

Yet Freire ([1970] 2000, 142) cautions that formal leadership development, even with good intentions, can foster isolation and dominance: "The same divisive effect occurs in connection with the so-called 'leadership training courses,' which are (although carried out without any such intention by many of the organizers) in the last analysis alienating. These courses are based on the naïve assumption that one can promote the community by training its leaders—as if it were the parts that promote the whole and not the whole which, in being promoted, promotes the parts." Freire is concerned that leaders in training will learn how to manipulate and control community members, which is antithetical to liberation. With this concern in mind, leadership programs must work against the temptation to create top-down trainings that reinforce the status quo. For instance, a program that teaches people how to adapt to rather than change oppressive policies and structures may simply reproduce exclusion, marginalization, and systemic harms.

A counterexample is the leadership academy described in the introduction of this chapter. During my listening tour as a new associate provost, I learned of the isolation some faculty and staff had experienced. I also learned about the lack of advancement opportunities, especially for staff and for women and people of color. Faculty and staff had great ideas for ways to create a more mission-aligned campus environment but little agency to test their hypotheses. Through the practice of *acompañamiento* and in observing the environments in which people worked, I came to learn that the new leadership academy needed to build bridges across functional areas (e.g., academic affairs and admissions), disciplines (e.g., medical school and humanities), and hierarchical levels (e.g., faculty and staff and administrative leadership). It also needed to provide knowledge about how the university worked so that people knew where to get information and how to plan change effectively. And the academy needed to demonstrate that we valued the expertise people brought to their work. The provost used an emergent change paradigm by setting the intention for improving faculty and staff quality of life and gave us a timeline for a launch.

I enlisted several faculty, staff, and administrative leaders to be on a steering committee to map out the experience. There was no way I could do this alone, not only because of the scope but also because I did not have a lock on the knowledge, skills, and format that would be most useful. The committee included representatives of the faculty and academic staff governance body, experts in leadership and management, and a representative from human resources. The committee was also diverse with respect to age, gender, and race. We decided to structure the academy as a fellowship. Fellows proposed and carried out a project to make life better for faculty, staff, or students. Fellows met once per month with the steering committee as cofacilitators to build skills (e.g., assessment, project management, budgeting) and move their projects forward. Fellows were also assigned a mentor and a sponsor to meet with regularly. Networking was integrated throughout the program so that fellows could learn from each other and find collaboration partners. After I left the university, the academy continued to adapt to the needs of participants. Fellows from prior years served as mentors and curriculum steering committee members. Additional sessions on vulnerability and psychological safety were added to acknowledge oppressive cultures and empower fellows to band together to effect change.

Fellows benefited from the program in many ways. They learned new skills, built their networks, completed worthwhile projects, and developed confidence in their leadership. But the benefits extended to others as well. The steering committee learned along with the fellows and experienced several aha moments when we discovered that our ideas were not the best ones after all. Mentors and sponsors benefited by being exposed to creative ideas from others they would not have worked with otherwise. The wider community benefited from the projects, which continue to enhance the university's educational offerings, student services, faculty and staff support, community engagement, and other domains. The community of liberatory leaders who can call on each other for support continues to grow.

This work was not without challenges and growing pains. For instance, some mentors and sponsors did not advocate effectively on behalf of their protégés or they tried to steer them toward their own pet projects. It was not enough to select mentors and sponsors with a groundskeeping mindset; we also needed to clarify our expectations for them to grow into these roles. We also realized that staff were faced with structural impediments to career growth. There were limited opportunities for them to advance given the structure of the units in which they worked. Many universities struggle with career advancement ladders, especially for staff. It is ideal if leadership development programs are accompanied by structural changes to allow for meaningful career progression for participants.

Developing full-blown academies like this can be difficult at institutions with limited resources or leadership churn, both of which may indicate that the timing is not right for a leadership development program. Yet there are still ways to craft development programs that fit your context. For example, I was able to adapt the leadership academy concept to a smaller institution by running a summer program for two to three faculty who were paid a stipend for their time and effort. They proposed and carried out collaborative projects aligned with the unit's priorities (e.g., creating an early-career mentoring program, crafting an inclusive webpage for faculty and staff recruitment). We met during the summer to discuss their projects and so I could connect them to other potential collaborators across the institution. They also chose a book on a higher education topic that we all read as part of a book group. In a smaller way, this program helped midcareer faculty flex their leadership skills, build a stronger network, and contribute to liberation at the university in a way that was meaningful to them.

Through your reading of reality and experience of *acompañamiento*, you have likely learned about the factors that are hampering or fostering liberatory change in your unit. As discussed in other parts of this book, people may need to first practice critical consciousness raising and self-reflection, reading reality at your institution, empathic listening, and courageous action as part of their leadership development. These skills can be developed as part of an intentional leadership training curriculum to dismantle oppression and gatekeeping at our institutions. Rather than simply giving people the keys to open the gate, leadership development can tear down the gate altogether and create a more welcoming entrance for everyone.

Holding Leaders Accountable

The CEBs used their collective power to advocate for and collaborate with leaders who advanced the cause of liberation. They also held leaders, within and outside the CEBs, accountable when they did not live up to liberatory ideals. The CEBs were growing the skills of leaders as they were also learning from leaders. This liberating praxis of mutual accountability continues to this day. In a similar way, academic leaders can promote liberation by inviting accountability for their own leadership and holding other leaders accountable as well. Accountability is an essential ingredient for growing liberatory skills throughout the system.

Assess Your Leadership

The formal evaluation of leaders is rare in higher education. I find this strange because colleges and universities are in the business of evaluation. Done well, assessment helps educators improve their teaching quality and effectiveness. Shouldn't leaders also desire feedback to improve their leadership? It is oppressive when administrative leaders require others to engage in evaluations but refuse to assess themselves. Liberatory leaders can act against this norm by inviting assessments of their leadership.

One option, used in business and now increasingly in higher education, is to conduct a 360-degree assessment. The assessment includes the supervisor, peer colleagues, and people who report to the leader. The leader selects 5–15 individuals across these categories. Respondents are asked to complete an anonymous survey or interview by an executive coach or other consultant about the leader's strengths and weaknesses. The coach provides summary feedback to the leader, protecting the confidentiality of the respondents. I have witnessed leaders improve their skills in transparent communication, organization, and collaboration after they participated in these assessments. The assessments can be self-serving, however, if the leader handpicks respondents who will give favorable reviews, if there is a lack of psychological safety that prevents others from telling the truth, or if the leader selectively attends to feedback that puts them in a positive light. Furthermore, 360s that simply ask about general leadership strengths and weaknesses are not necessarily serving liberation. To infuse liberation into a 360, include questions about liberatory leadership skills such as critical self-reflection, *acompañamiento*, and empowering others to lead change. Coaches can then follow up with respondents to learn more about specific behaviors that can be eliminated or added to the leaders' repertoires in service of liberation. Additionally, care must be taken to ensure that coaches and supervisors are aware of oppressive biases that may infiltrate survey responses. For instance, comments that appear to denigrate or police the tone of leaders need to be interpreted in light of sexism, racism, anti-Semitism, Islamophobia, and other systems of oppression. Carefully choose the questions and interpret the results based on the reality of the institution, including how leaders from marginalized communities are generally perceived.

Although they can offer useful information, a drawback to 360s is that they are not designed to account for sentiment in larger units. Critics may discount the usefulness of a 360 that consists of respondents selected by the leader, and for good reason: tenure and promotion procedures do not often allow candidates to select their review committees or outside letter writers. And faculty cannot sample just a few students when they do teaching evaluations. Why would we evaluate leaders differently? For this reason, it may be a good option to survey everyone in your unit. As with the 360, consider including items that can tap into liberatory behaviors and skills. In one of my positions, we did not have a budget to pay for surveys by third-party vendors, so I created items derived from Salwa Rahim-Dillard's (2021) article entitled "How Inclusive Is Your Leadership?" Some of the items were, "This leader models authenticity, vulnerability, and openness," and, "This leader speaks out and acts against injustice, exclusion, and inequity." Faculty and staff responded to each item on a Likert-type scale ranging from "strongly disagree" to "strongly agree." I also added open-ended questions to learn how my team and I could better serve their needs in the coming year. The anonymous survey was then distributed by another office. Not everyone stayed on topic; some used the open-ended questions to express other concerns. But I was able to track how the group as a whole perceived my leadership year over year. I was able to identify areas of strength and skills in which I fell short. I then reported the results and the actions I planned to take in response to the results to everyone in the unit. My transparency and action helped cultivate honest and open discussion about what my job was, where I was growing, and what I should continue to do to lead the unit. Not only was I open to accountability, I was holding myself accountable.

One thing I was not able to do was disaggregate the data with an intersectional lens. I simply did not have enough representation in my unit to break down responses by race, gender, and other identities without revealing the identities of some faculty and staff. If you have a critical mass of diversity, examine patterns across respondents with diverse lived experiences, especially people who experience multiple marginalizations (e.g., Black women) (Scott, 2021; Malhotra, 2022). If, like me, you are not able to do this, consider using your listening tour as another way to collect information about your leadership. You may also find that sharing the results will generate additional feedback that you would not have received otherwise. For instance, after I shared the results of my survey, several faculty of color and their allies reached out to me in solidarity regarding vitriolic comments about my inclusive vision. They encouraged me to continue doing what I was doing.

The thought of receiving feedback from an entire unit can be anxiety provoking, which may partly explain why this is not done more often in higher education. It may be helpful to cultivate an "inclusion mindset" (Malhotra, 2022, 41). Borrowing from Carol Dweck's (2006) concept of a growth mindset, an inclusion mindset demonstrates a willingness to learn and make mistakes about inclusion. To develop this mindset, Ruchika Malhotra recommends inviting feedback, holding defensiveness at bay, and growing from our mistakes. Being open to what other people think about our leadership helps us move forward. It also helps to model courage for other leaders who can grow from feedback.

Hold Others Accountable

Growing liberatory skills in others requires that we hold other leaders accountable. Yet because assessment of higher education leadership is not the norm, even the discussion of evaluating others' leadership capacity may be scary. If you have people who report to you, your human resources office may already have performance evaluation processes for staff. Faculty leaders, however, have few avenues for formal leadership feedback. If you supervise faculty or staff who supervise others, invite their ideas for how to best assess their leadership. Learn whether questions can be added to existing assessments to reinforce liberatory leadership, or at the very least DEI. If leadership assessments are not yet a practice, however, consider introducing evaluations gradually. As a new dean, I learned that department chairs submitted annual reports about their departments' challenges and achievements. To this annual report, I added several self-reflection questions to begin supporting leaders in their own development. Questions included, "What gifts, talents, or skills do you bring to your department/program leadership?" "How has serving in this role been personally fulfilling to you?" and, "How has serving in this role been frustrating or draining?" In a subsequent conversation, we discussed their roles as leaders (not just managers) and their aspirations. This conversation was intended to convey that I cared about their development as faculty leaders. It also helped me understand the reality of their experiences and how I could back them up as they took risks, including speaking out about injustice. Chairs' reactions to the assessment and follow-up conversation helped me further learn about their leadership challenges. For instance, some were just keeping their heads above water because of the sheer number of tasks in front of them. The work of liberation seemed overwhelming when there were so many things to get done. In those cases, supporting them meant having conversations with them and with other leaders around the university about lightening the load. Assessment in this case not only helped change the conversation about leadership but also helped us begin cocreating a different reality for leaders and those they served.

Because of our commitment to liberating systems, we must also attend to situations in which leaders hamper the growth of others. If the missteps are not egregious and you perceive that it is possible for someone to improve, apply an inclusion mindset to provide feedback, ask for corrective action, and assess whether it is taken. Kim Scott (2021) writes that the consequences should match the types of problematic behaviors in the workplace. For instance, when people operate from unaware bias, then education is needed. When people are aware of their prejudices and still act from them, then a code of conduct (e.g., a rule for engagement) is needed to prevent this behavior in the future. And when people engage in bullying, clear consequences are a must. Scott offers various tactics depending on whether people are targets, observers or "upstanders," or perpetrators. She also offers ideas for how leaders can set the tone for a more just workplace culture, including a code of conduct that clearly articulates acceptable and unacceptable behaviors. In academic circles, we might call these community agreements. In fact, it is surprising that many faculty have community agreements for their classes but do not adopt a similar strategy to hold each other accountable. I have encountered some faculty and staff who are fortunate to work in relatively healthy units and are resistant to creating community agreements because of the time it will take. But this is the best time to work on accountability. It is better to put guidelines in place for the future when things are going well than when discord and harm are occurring.

Counter Oppressive Narratives

Liberatory leaders publicly counter narratives that prevent liberation from taking root. For instance, academic leadership searches can be aimed at selecting leaders who are motivated and rewarded to free up academic cultures so that everyone can thrive. Yet a common refrain during these searches goes something like this: "We want someone who has done this before. If they've held this title before, they must know what they are doing." This is an oppressive narrative because it restricts the pool of eligible candidates; leadership skews increasingly white and male as one progresses up the organizational chart at many colleges and universities (Caño, 2023). Therefore, stating that successful candidates will have already been provost or president, for example, increases the likelihood that the person who is hired is a white man. Rather than tacitly accept this state of affairs, try to identify the reasons behind this desire and ask questions out loud for others to witness. Perhaps there is an assumption that people in a similar role have the skills to be successful. What are those skills specifically? How might people have acquired these skills in other roles and experiences? How will prematurely restricting the pool based on title go against the diversity goals set by the institution? How does the expectation that new leaders must know everything there is to know about leadership align with academia's expectations that our students will engage in lifelong learning? Sometimes these questions will have no seeming effect on the final decision. But countering narratives with questions can grow liberatory skills in others who observe your courage in publicly opposing oppressive narratives so that they start asking questions themselves.

At times, you can invite others into your own story to oppose internalized narratives of oppressive leadership. Doing so can help emerging leaders to shed oppressive expectations about how they might "do" leadership. As an example, I once attended a university-sponsored talk by a Latina leader in a male-dominated industry whose internalized sexism, racism, and colonial mentality created a harmful narrative for students, especially Latinas. The speaker described her rise to the top of her field as an act of will, hard work, and persistence, never acknowledging cultural strengths that enabled her to persist or cultural obstacles. She advised students to stick to their goals no matter what because too many women dropped out along the way. Her responses to students' direct questions flew in the face of their experiences of racism and sexism in college and in society. After checking in with others, I came to respect that she was a "first" in her field, that her attitudes were likely self-protective, but I also recognized that students were demoralized by this narrative. I realized as well that the students might benefit from an alternative view. A Latine student group invited me to their meeting and asked me to share my leadership journey with them. They asked if I ever felt like a failure, whether I experienced sexism and racism as a leader, and if I ever wanted to quit. I shared a resounding yes to all three questions. I also explained that I gather strength from my cultural and family upbringing, my current community, and successes and so-called failures along the way. I hoped to provide a liberating counternarrative for this next generation of leaders.

Summary

Growing liberatory skills in others is necessary to create a critical mass of leaders at all levels who can collaborate to change the culture. Leaders who cultivate the liberation ecosystem seed culture change while also being transformed by those they lead. Liberating actions like developing the leadership of others have potential to convert traditional hierarchical relationships into partnerships that cocreate a new reality. This is hard work. To persist, leaders need to safeguard their peace so they stay true to their values and maintain the energy needed to persist in the cause of liberation.

Question for Reflection and Action

- How would making a choice to nurture liberatory leadership in others support culture change at your institution?
- How did you learn about the hidden curriculum of academic leadership? How can you reveal it to others to support systemic liberation?
- Analyze the composition of your network. To what extent does your network consist of people with diverse lived experiences? What can you do to expand your network?

- How comfortable are you serving as a sponsor? Have you sponsored women across races or people across genders? What did you learn?
- How can you practice emergent leadership in the teams you lead or facilitate?
- What are some ways you can contribute a liberatory perspective to leadership development at your institution?
- How might you make liberating changes to how your leadership is assessed?

CHAPTER 7

Safeguarding Your Peace

My father moved across the country to live at an assisted living facility close to my family during what was a stressful time in my career. In the span of eight months, his health declined precipitously. As the only family member nearby, I was the point person for emergency room visits, late-night phone calls, and medical decisions (thankfully, my sister handled finances from afar). My father eventually entered hospice care, then passed away peacefully. Going through this while serving in a demanding leadership role and attempting to be a supportive spouse and mother was trying and stressful. I gained weight from eating and drinking my stress, and I began having more frequent headaches and back pain. I pushed through all that needed to be done at work and home. Around this time, my son said, "When Dad and I hear you muttering under your breath, we know to leave you alone." It was at once humorous and mortifying. If I was going to have the energy to support liberation at work (which is hard enough during good times) and be there for my family, I needed to cultivate and safeguard my inner peace.

The work of liberating systems and accompanying others in solidarity requires stamina. There will be times when we are disappointed or disheartened by learning about the challenges experienced by others. And we will undoubtedly be blocked and even experience failure from time to time when we act courageously. Added to this, other aspects of our lives require and deserve our time, concentration, and socio-emotional-spiritual energy. Throughout my life, I have had to relearn how important it is to protect my peace if I want to be a liberating force at work, an engaged citizen, and a supportive mom, spouse, sister, and friend. I am no good when I spread myself too thin. Pushing through might be a temporary solution but long term, this strategy can do damage not only to our bodies but to our spirits. It also reinforces and models to others unhealthy norms of overwork and overcommitment. Ultimately, acquiescing to grind culture in this way undermines our ability to participate in liberation.

In this chapter, I explore not only how oppressive workplaces disturb our peace and drain our energy but how to resist and actively replenish our energy. We must use our observational skills to read the reality of our situations. Then we can take steps to safeguard our peace by setting boundaries, curating joy, reframing, and preparing for the future. It is imperative that leaders do what they can to replenish and protect their energy reserves as part of liberation praxis. If we do not take the time to intentionally safeguard our peace, we will experience bitterness, burnout, and defeat. We succumb to oppression rather than resist it. Let's develop habits that enable others to safeguard their own peace and engage in liberating action.

What Drains Our Energy

Ruchika Malhotra (2022) notes that unexamined exclusionary practices disproportionately harm women of color. Academia is no exception. A host of practices and norms create oppressive working environments, especially for those who historically have been excluded from higher education: expectations to "publish or perish" for tenure-stream faculty, faculty-staff hierarchies and inequalities, a grind culture of contingent teaching work, and the emphasis on following the "chain of command" for requests and complaints. Oppressive academic culture sets the stage for specific behaviors and expectations that chip away at our energy reserves, making us more vulnerable to giving up and allowing the status quo to go unchallenged. This is exactly what the system was designed to do.

Meeting Culture

Oppressive meeting behaviors drain faculty and staff of the time, energy, and spirit required to engage in liberatory work. In my experience, it is a common practice to expect folks to attend meetings that do not require their participation. Obligatory face time at meetings takes away valuable time and energy that could have been better used to get things done. Last-minute meeting requests can also be destabilizing and stressful. One semester, meetings were added to my calendar on days I had booked vacation time. The conveners did not know that I planned to take the day off; they simply assumed everyone was available every day that was not a university holiday. Along with the invite came the acknowledgment that although the time didn't work for everyone, we should make every effort to attend. What a message!

Poorly run meetings with no agenda can also deplete our energy and allow hostilities and microaggressions to irritate and tire us out.

Accompaniment Without Boundaries

In addition to unhealthy meeting culture, the very act of accompaniment can turn oppressive, coming at the expense of our peace. The reality is that in any leadership position, there is simply not enough time to deal with every concern or issue that needs to be addressed every day; and that's not even factoring in the unexpected and urgent matters and crises that require immediate intervention. On top of obligations during normal business hours, some leaders may need to attend performances, athletic and recruitment events, and other activities in the evenings and on weekends. But there is only so much time to take care of everything, including health-care appointments, quality time with family and friends, and other activities.

When leaders enter environments in which people are thirsty for liberatory leadership, the challenge of accompaniment can be particularly tricky, especially for leaders who do not fit the "ideal worker" norm—the ever-available full-time employee who has no caregiving or housework responsibilities (J. Williams, 2001). For the majority of us who do not fit this norm, we have all the paperwork, meetings, projects, and events plus an expectation to be ever available to others. There is no time or grace allowed for what happens outside work. If we are not mindful, this situation can set us up for an unhealthy workload or anger from others when we set limits on our time.

Finally, our work can be especially stressful or draining depending on our personal identities and life experiences. For instance, it can be draining to hold others accountable for exclusionary and marginalizing behavior that we ourselves have experienced. In one particular stretch of my academic leadership work, I had educational conversations with several different male faculty about appropriate language and behavior toward women students. In most of the cases, the faculty reacted with defensiveness and outrage at the perceived injustice that had been done to them. In some of the cases, I also picked up an unspoken resentment toward me as the woman leader giving them feedback. Though unpleasant, I knew that providing candid feedback was important to protect those with less power, and I did my best to deliver the information with compassion. But that doesn't mean that it was easy. I was emotionally spent after each one of those conversations.

These are just a few examples of how oppressive academic culture can diminish our capacity to engage in the socio-emotional-spiritual work of liberating action. We experience a variety of ill consequences when we allow oppressive culture and practices to drain us: lost relationships, poor health, disengagement, and burnout.

Burnout: A Serious Consequence of Oppression

Rebecca Pope-Ruark (2022) explains that academia's capitalistic, patriarchal culture fosters unhealthy competition, excessive reward seeking, and a culture of burnout that disproportionately affects women faculty. I still recall my surprise years ago when

I asked a faculty mentee if she had enjoyed her winter vacation. I knew she often burned the candle at both ends and I hoped she had gotten some rest. She responded by telling me about the grants and manuscripts she worked on and how little sleep she got. She took pride in her work ethic. In her mind, this was the formula for success and survival. I understood why she was telling me, a tenured faculty member who might review her promotion and tenure package, how hard she worked. But I also felt sad because I had been trying to model a healthier balance and I was publicly urging others in my department to do the same. Pope-Ruark (2022, 7) captures this internalized oppression: "We would wear it as a badge of honor to feel included in the cult of busyness that has cursed so many of us to fetishize productivity and reputation, not questioning the systemic structures feeding this perspective."

Pope-Ruark draws from the World Health Organization's International Classification of Diseases and the work of Christina Maslach and colleagues (2001) to describe burnout as a set of symptoms that include severe exhaustion, mental detachment from or cynicism about one's work, and a sense that one is ineffective or accomplishing little at work. Maslach and her colleagues' research demonstrates that workplace burnout is caused by excessive workloads, lack of agency over one's work, and a mismatch between one's values and the values of the organization. Unchecked academic burnout can lead to a host of adverse physical and psychological consequences that affect not only the burned-out individual but their colleagues, students, and loved ones. In chronicling her own and other women's experiences, Pope-Ruark recommends that individuals be empowered to make choices that support their own health, meaning making, and vitality. She also urges people to work on collectively changing expectations for women in academia and making systemic changes that counter prevailing norms of overwork and productivity.

As liberatory leaders, we have the responsibility and the privilege to cocreate culture change with others so that everyone, especially the most marginalized and excluded among us, avoids being burned out by academia. Helping to safeguard others' peace is part of liberatory work. So is protecting our own peace as leaders. If we lose ourselves to the quest for success as defined by an oppressive culture and our peers who subscribe to this culture, we will burn out too. We deserve better as human beings. Whether or not you have the authority or a critical mass of liberatory coconspirators with whom to shift the culture, you can take measures to safeguard your peace. Use your keen observational skills to read and respond to reality, collaborate with others to cocreate new cultures, and make individual and collective course corrections.

Observe the Cues

Lillian Comas-Díaz (2022, 313) writes, "Combatting oppression can be oppressive—if you don't take care of yourself." But before we can take care of ourselves, we need to recognize our limits.

Listen to Your Body

Our bodies are pretty good at telling us what we might not already know. Yet we don't always want to listen. In one job I loved, I had to navigate around leaders who were insecure and did whatever they could to hold on to their power and authority. As I continued in this position, I began having migraine headaches and severe back pain. One day, a colleague took me aside to ask why I stayed if my body was telling me so clearly that I needed to leave. One answer was that I did not want to come to terms with the truth. But my body knew the truth all along. When I announced my departure from my job, I felt an enormous weight lifted even as I was angry that I had to give up the values-driven work I was doing. Since then, I have had to remind myself that rest is required for me to safeguard my peace. When work and stress creep into my rest times, then I know I need to double down on "reclaiming my time," in the immortal words of US congresswoman Maxine Waters (D-CA).

Listen to Yourself

There are many ways to pay attention to your own inner reactions as you move through the world: regular journaling or wellness apps can help identify patterns in your thoughts and feelings, including when you are starting to slide into unhealthy habits. Note the kinds of activities, events, or interpersonal interactions that energize you and those that deplete you. Reflect on your mood as you go through the day to determine whether you are moving toward or away from liberating action for yourself and with others. Track how safeguarding your peace correlates with your mood and energy levels.

In some cases, changes in mood that interfere with your daily life may signal that it is time to consult a health professional. Contact a therapist if your responses (or those of your loved ones) reveal that you have lost interest in things you once found enjoyable; you feel depressed, down, or anxious for most of the day nearly every day; or you have thoughts or intentions of harming yourself or others. Recognize that seeking health and wellness for yourself is healing and liberatory work.

Listen to Others

After the episode when my son told me about my mumbling, I tried to become more aware of my stress levels and what I was radiating at home. A colleague of mine shared a similar story with me. Her child would tell siblings, "Stay away from Mama because she's in a bad mood!" Loved ones and trusted colleagues may notice things before you do. Listen to them and learn where you might need to make adjustments to protect your peace and theirs as well.

Set Liberating Boundaries

When my father's health was declining, I was fortunate to work at an institution that emphasized care for the whole person. When I shared how difficult it was to juggle the many demands on my time and psyche, I received many an encouraging word. When my father passed away, there was an outpouring of support that I appreciate to this day. Yet despite this sentiment, I was still expected to show up and get work done in a timely fashion and to be as available as I ever was. This expectation to be "always on" is not healthy, even when things are going well in our personal lives. No matter the culture, we can benefit from setting firmer boundaries at work.

Liberate Your Calendar

If you are a leader with some authority to do so, set limits on your calendar so that you have enough time, energy, and mental capacity to carry out your liberatory work. Say yes to events that are aligned with your valued priorities and be transparent when you decline. Let people know the reasons why you cannot hit every event. Model authenticity and integrity by disclosing if you have other obligations at that time. For instance, perhaps you would love to attend but you cannot because of caregiving responsibilities. Sharing this reason allows others to do the same. You may be able to ask another member of your team to attend to show that the office values the work put into the event. You may also be able to send good wishes before and after the event if you cannot attend. Check in with trusted colleagues to learn about the commitments that you surely cannot miss. Listen to yourself as well to detect when other people's "must attend" events are aligned with your values as a liberatory leader.

Besides events, committee work and meetings can chew up time on our calendar. Granted, it is important that we have seats at various tables where we can offer a liberatory vision, build partnerships, and advocate for our units. It is also the case that leaders are often asked to serve on committees because of the power and authority we represent, not because our input will be used. In some academic cultures, the tradition of inviting leaders with positional power despite its limited usefulness goes unquestioned. Ask why you are being invited and what the convener hopes to gain by your participation. If you judge that your specific participation is not necessary but someone else is prepared to contribute, then recommend that they attend instead.

A caveat about delegating: refrain from contributing to unhealthy workloads through excessive delegation. Studies have shown that faculty with marginalized identities provide more invisible labor—labor that is not recognized for promotion purposes (e.g., advising students of color)—than those with dominant identities (Social Sciences Feminist Network Research Interest Group, 2017). Leaders can help address this disparity by paying attention to whom they delegate to. KerryAnn O'Meara and colleagues (2017) showed that women were asked to do new work, including committee service, more frequently than men. A conversation with potential delegates before any opportunities arise can help you identify people who have the bandwidth and interest to participate. Also seek out those for whom the activity is aligned with their values and who may benefit from the participation in terms of networking or skill building.

Leaders from marginalized communities are under the microscope and may be hypervisible, for better or worse. One year, I missed a large university celebration because I prioritized an event at my child's school. I was worried about what people would think when they noticed my absence. But people swore they saw me there! Isis Settles, NiCole Buchanan, and Kristie Dotson (2019) explain that faculty of color who are tokenized because they signal diversity are likely to experience this hypervisibility. The perception of hypervisibility can also lead to hurt feelings. One semester, students blamed me for not attending events that I was not invited to. They assumed that as a woman leader of color, I would know all that was going on when it had to do with marginalized communities. In this case, I was able to have conversations with students about the other pressures on my calendar, including the need for rest and time with my family in the evenings and on weekends, when most of the student events were scheduled. My transparency helped clear up the miscommunication and set healthier expectations. I was also able to show my support in other ways, which helped them realize that I valued their work even if I could not be present.

Free Up Meeting Time

Liberatory leaders can accompany others while also protecting their own time and peace by how they run meetings. Steven Rogelberg (2019) offers a number of suggestions to prepare and facilitate meetings, some of which stand out as particularly liberatory because they free people to participate fully in meetings and use their time wisely. For instance, observe people's in-meeting behaviors to assess the extent to which everyone engages, feels free to express divergent viewpoints, and stays on topic. Use your observation skills during the meeting and ask participants how they experienced the meeting afterward. You may learn that the meeting could have been shorter or that you need to work on your facilitation skills to lead a meeting worth having. As much as possible, set meeting agendas ahead of time. For one-on-ones, request that your direct reports share their agenda some time in advance. I typically asked for an agenda 24 hours before the meeting so I could mentally prepare for the conversation. If I had anything to add, I would let my meeting partner know about it ahead of time, if possible.

Also pay attention to why people are seeking one-on-one meetings with you. At one point in my career, people left our meetings saying, "I always feel better after talking to you." I was flattered. At the same time, it led to too many meeting requests; it became difficult for me to find time to read proposals, think, and craft strategy. For some of these meeting requests, there was no overt agenda. The hidden agenda was that my meeting partner wanted to feel better about something. It was not lost on me that my identity as a Latina and my professional skills as a psychologist and spiritual director may have played into other people's expectations of me as a caregiver. Whereas accompaniment is part of being a liberatory leader, it may be time to do some introspection and set healthy boundaries with others if the primary and recurring reason they want a meeting is to feel better.

For group meetings, Rogelberg recommends inviting input on creating the agenda. This strategy may take several attempts if oppressive leadership has been the rule. Participants need to learn that they are truly collaborators and not just followers. This strategy can protect your peace because it allows you to prepare for meetings and limits the adrenaline surges that come with surprises. Of course, this works only if team members trust that they are true partners in the work and you are not paying lip service to their ideas. There may be times when a suggestion is off topic or better discussed in a different venue. If that's the case, do not ignore the suggestion. Share with the team member your thoughts about the potential agenda item and seek their input about other ways it can be addressed or discussed.

When you are invited to join a committee or a meeting, ask questions beforehand so you can make wise decisions about your participation. "Thanks for the invitation. What are you hoping I can contribute by being part of this meeting, group, or committee?" Sometimes the leader needs to be there to make decisions or give the go-ahead for an initiative to proceed. But other times, we are asked to attend when it actually doesn't matter or because of tradition. And then there are times when we are asked to be present so other leaders can shield themselves from challenges or difficult questions from other participants. Before saying yes to any of these invitations, let the requester know that you need some time to weigh this invitation against your other obligations. This can get a little tricky when someone with greater positional power asks you to participate. But you can still ask questions so that you have full knowledge about your role and responsibilities before agreeing to add something to your calendar.

Communicate Your Values

Setting boundaries as a liberatory leader requires clear communication lest others misread your intentions. For instance, stating that you do not send or receive emails on weekends unless it's an emergency may be interpreted by people who have internalized oppressive work norms as a lack of dedication to your work. Consider explaining that your email policy is aimed at creating healthier work environments for everyone. If this does not make sense to the other leader, then share how protecting your time and peace allows you to feel refreshed and ready to tackle work when you return.

Be Prepared for Pushback

One of my managers responded to my request that they refrain from emailing on weekends with a sarcastic smirk and continued their practice of emailing on the weekends until enough other people made the same request. At the very least, you can institute a healthy email policy with anyone who reports to you. If you are fortunate to have an assistant or a team, they can help communicate your value-infused boundaries so that the practice spreads more widely. You can also band together with colleagues to collectively reset expectations and safeguard each other's peace.

Think about other ways you can communicate your values to set healthy boundaries at work. For instance, is it really OK that everyone has your cell phone number or that they can text you anytime they want? Some of us need to be on call because of our duties (e.g., student affairs, health care, campus security), but most of us do not have the responsibility to be available at all hours. One faculty member told me that whenever there was university news, the group text chat for the department would light up, interrupting their concentration and ability to focus. In this case, turning off the group chats and declining new invitations may have helped them protect their peace.

Similarly, be mindful of the oppressive power of gossip. Gossip is a hot commodity in academia, in part, because we are in the business of knowledge production and transmission. It is also a sign of an oppressive, hierarchical system that limits transparency and creates information vacuums. It is hard to turn off the gossip machine, but it is possible to limit your exposure. Directly communicate your values about cocreating healthier environments by stating that you want to protect people's privacy or refrain from spreading news about others that is not yours to tell.

Rest

Rest is the unsung hero of setting limits. In her book *Rest Is Resistance: A Manifesto* (2022), Tricia Hersey writes that capitalism and white supremacy have created a grind culture that forces us to sacrifice our health and well-being. In cultures of overwork and urgency, the body is the site of liberation. Rest creates a moment of freedom. Pope-Ruark (2022) also prescribes rest as a way to set humane boundaries with our work identities. None of us is any good to anyone, including our loved ones, if we're exhausted and burned out.

There are many ways to rest. The most obvious is to get more sleep at night. As a health psychologist, I worked with many people on how to prepare and train their bodies to sleep: for instance, avoid caffeine and strenuous exercise, refrain from using technology that emits blue light, and limit one's exposure to emotionally charged material before bed. Hersey also recommends naps during the day as radical rest. For those who protest that they cannot nap, Hersey begs to differ. She counters that this attitude comes from internalized messages that rest is a sign of laziness, especially for Black people in countries that benefited from their enslavement and commodification. She writes that in capitalistic cultures, "rest is resistance." She also reassures us that we can train ourselves to wake up refreshed and ready for what's next. It takes practice but it's possible.

In addition to sleep, contemplative activities can revive our bodies, minds, and spirits. Taking a refreshing walk in the woods, sitting in the sunshine, meditating and praying, practicing yoga, and creating or enjoying art and music can all be restful practices. So can socializing with loved ones and seeking *acompañamiento* for yourself. Engaging in any of these activities means setting limits on the time and energy we devote to work. It also means setting limits with others who have internalized oppressive or toxic cultures and expect us to fall in line. To these trapped people, rest and leisure are "nice to haves" but they have no real purpose. Liberatory leaders realize rest is required to continue to resist and dismantle oppression.

How do we make time for rest when there is so much pressure against it? Use your calendars to reserve days or blocks of time for vacation and rest. While I recommend that you be ruthless with these blocks, it is a good idea to have a backup plan if something interferes. For instance, you or a loved one may become ill and need care, or a supervisor may call an urgent meeting that truly requires your participation. One of my backup strategies involved replacing time whenever it was taken away from me. For instance, for every blocked hour that I had to give up for something else, I tried to block an additional hour that week or the following week. When I was successful in pulling this off, not only did I have the time and energy to get things done in a healthy state of mind, but I also felt a sense of agency that buoyed my spirit. If you have the privilege of an assistant who manages your calendar, ask them to help defend your time, and return the favor.

Then follow through. Use the blocked time to take that rest. Almost every leader I've ever talked to has disclosed that they never used all their vacation days. They also plowed through times during their workday that they had originally blocked for rest. We are made to feel like we cannot take breaks because there is too much work to do. A wise colleague once told me that the work is infinite but our lives are finite. So if you earn vacation days in your position, take them! If you feel inner resistance, think critically about how the culture in your unit contributes to this feeling. Interrogate yourself. Are you attached to the image of being that person who is so dedicated, you never take time off? How does this align with your values of liberation?

Get creative if you cannot block out time for rest during the workday. Schedule meetings with a 5- or 10-minute buffer at the beginning or the end (e.g., block out a 60-minute timeslot for a 50-minute meeting) to allow for a mental and emotional breather between meetings. Use your lunchtime or even travel time to meetings to move around, listen to music, or engage in your preferred rest activity. Make space before or after work for activities that allow you to rest. If you use mass transit on your commute, use that time to rest rather than do more work.

Finally, if you can, get away. I was surprised that attending a higher education conference after a particularly grueling semester was so beneficial to my mental health. Not only was I able to bring back useful knowledge to benefit my institution, but my empty tank was filled by the interactions with lovely colleagues. It felt like rest. I joked with my supervisor that they could retain me by sending me away periodically. Professional development, including leaves and sabbaticals (Caño, 2024), can be restful if we are intentional about how we spend this time. Unplugged spiritual or self-care retreats also provide opportunities to rest and reconnect with what is important. Restful times away allow us to engage in the creative and expansive thinking to envision *un otro mundo posible*.

Curate Joy

In their essay "Administrative Joy" (2022), Karlyn Crowley and Jay Roberts observe that higher education administrative leaders are expected to put up with criticism, challenges, and stress without complaint. But as they put it, "we all need to feel joy to do our jobs well." Crowley and Roberts recommend that we engage in activities that remind us of our purpose and mission (e.g., mingle with students), find like-minded colleagues to share our ups and downs, and use humor to get us through dark times.

Crowley and Roberts also make an excellent suggestion to cultivate joy by saving thank-you and other positive notes, cards, and emails from colleagues and students. Take the time to read them when you receive them and save them for the rainy days that are indeed in the future. The Jesuits, including the Salvadoran martyrs who inspired this book, refer to this practice of storing up consolations as "savoring." Savor the experiences that bring joy, hope, and love. Do not let the opportunity to sit with these consolations pass you by because of a sense of urgency or an attitude that minimizes their importance. Celebrate the small wins! It may also help to keep a list of small and big wins in a file to review on those days you feel like you have not accomplished anything. Include hidden accomplishments like conversations that enabled you to continue the work of liberation.

Joy also comes from purposeful connection with others. Community building is an act of resistance. Find your people at your institution so you can support each other through *acompañamiento* and reality checking. Find your people in your discipline or who hold similar positions at other institutions to debrief in a confidential setting and share liberating ideas. And find your people in your community, outside academia, to build authentic friendships that are not dependent on rank, title, or what you can "do" for each other. Connections like these counter cultures of burnout and competition by favoring cultures that liberate us to play and enjoy the gifts others bring to our relationships.

I acknowledge that this is a difficult ask because it may feel like it creates more work; it takes time to go out and meet people. I can also attest that it is worth it. The day before I moved across the country for my dean job during the height of the pandemic, I met via Zoom with my four "COVID dean" counterparts in our university network. We were all external hires who signed our contracts before the pandemic struck, and each of us held one or more historically marginalized identities in academic leadership. I am grateful that we all made time for that initial meeting because our group ended up gathering regularly to compare notes, collaborate, commiserate, and laugh. It was a life-giving relationship in the midst of great upheaval and stress in our personal lives, at our institutions, and in the world.

Reframe

Reframing, or thinking about your situation differently, can make a big difference in carrying out liberatory work. If you think that blocking time for rest is selfish or self-centered, it will be more difficult to keep that time blocked when someone else wants it. But if you reframe blocked time as an appointment with yourself, you may be more likely to keep it. Wouldn't you be angry, or at the very least disappointed, if someone did not show up for an appointment with you? You can also take a lesson from writing coaches who reframe writing time as appointments with collaborators or with your audience. In this case, your blocked time is like an appointment with the colleagues who will benefit from you feeling well rested.

Delegation is also sometimes difficult for leaders in oppressive environments because it feels like the weight of the world has been placed on our shoulders. But thoughtfully assigning or delegating projects to others is not offloading work irresponsibly. Can you reframe "offloading" to "offering" a professional development opportunity to others who would like to grow? You may also be able to reframe how saying yes to everything may be harming your own growth. Accepting every new opportunity or assignment takes time away from your ability to engage in other liberatory activities, including rest. Be choosy and align your yesses with your mission.

Reframing can also be used to build stamina when you receive pushback. I recall a meeting when I described how disappointed I was with pushback about a diversity initiative I led. One of the faculty participants replied that we were not doing anything worthwhile if there was no pushback; if everyone felt comfortable, then we were supporting the status quo. That reframing resonated with the entire group and allowed us to forge on. Reframing does not change the situation when feedback about liberatory culture change is vitriolic, especially toward leaders with marginalized identities. It makes our work a bit easier, however, by providing distance from other people's heightened emotions. Family therapist Edwin Friedman (2007), in *A Failure of Nerve*, names this a hallmark practice of a "self-differentiated leader," someone who can take care of themselves without getting sucked into other people's disturbances.

Prepare for Stressors

Safeguarding your peace means knowing when situations are most likely to be stressful or chaotic. For many faculty, the beginning of the semester or quarter is hectic. For staff, it may be application deadlines, student orientations, or other annual deadlines. When you expect stress to ramp up, not just for you but for others as well, prepare by cutting back on meetings, additional assignments, or other activities that can be delayed. Allow space on your calendar for unexpected things in work and life in order to prevent overwork.

Prepare also by knowing the kind of feedback that pushes your buttons. For me, gendered comments that I am too compassionate almost always rub me the wrong way even though I am fully aware of the research showing that women leaders are often perceived as either warm or competent, but not both. Feedback like, "Enough with the Hugger in Chief, we need strong leadership!" (this is an actual comment I received on my annual anonymous leadership survey) presumes I cannot be competent if I am empathetic. Because I know I am triggered by this kind of comment, I can prepare by reminding myself about the research. I can also remind myself that compassionate leadership is strong leadership because it requires deep empathy, tolerance for ambiguity, and action—all of which require inner strength. In addition, I find it helpful to seek support from understanding others. In this case, one of my team members suggested we make T-shirts that said, "I stand with the Hugger in Chief!" While we didn't go that far, the humor and care in that comment sustained me in the moment. I also tucked that image away to refer to when I get similar feedback again.

Safeguard the Peace of Others

As you safeguard your peace, you will notice that others need accompaniment to safeguard their own peace. Not only is this helpful to them as individuals, but this practice can cocreate a culture of healthy peacekeeping for everyone. The following are some ideas to support others so they have the energy reserves to continue freeing up systems of oppression at work.

Be Mindful of Sharing Feedback

Assessment and evaluation are expected activities in academia; we want to ensure our work produces valued outcomes, so we need to measure, learn, and change our behavior as needed. Leaders are in the position of sharing feedback with colleagues about their performance, curriculum, or projects. But this does not mean that we need to share feedback that is sexist, racist, or otherwise harmful under the guise of transparent operations. As an act of accompaniment, check in with colleagues about what they prefer that you do if you receive unconstructive or harmful feedback about them as leaders. I had to learn this lesson the hard way.

After the release of a campus diversity, equity, and inclusion initiative, several people came to me to complain about it. In addition to specific concerns about the initiative itself, they made sexist and racist comments about the initiative's leader, a woman of the global majority. In the interest of transparency, I shared the entire list of comments with my colleague. She appreciated that she could rectify some misconceptions about the initiative, but she also shared that it was unnecessary and hurtful for me to include the harmful comments. I felt awful, apologized, and learned from my mistake of choosing transparency for transparency's sake. It is true that some leaders may want the full scoop. But others will only want and need the actionable items so they can keep focused on their work. Before providing feedback, ask your colleagues about their preferred format for receiving feedback (e.g., verbal, written) and whether they want everything, even if it includes harmful comments. Even better, cocreate guidelines and policies about appropriate feedback along with consequences for providing harmful feedback.

Safeguarding Others Versus Transparency

When and how we share information with others also matters when safeguarding others' peace. Sometimes, sharing every bit of information in real time is unnecessarily anxiety provoking. Take, for example, the process of faculty recruitment, which can elicit fears about lost lines if the search "fails." As the hiring manager who negotiated with faculty candidates on behalf of the university, it was tempting for me to let the search committee chair know immediately when a top candidate had another job offer. Telling the committee right away could support my desire to be transparent with search committees, whose members were often anxious for information because of the heightened competition among schools for a limited pool of candidates. But the fact of the matter was that the chair could not act on this information to change the situation. All they could do was worry about losing their top candidate, and spread that anxiety to others. This was not a good use of their time or emotional energy because they had many other responsibilities. Instead, I learned to share updates when I also could share a plan (e.g., enhance their start-up package) and a timeline, or when I sought input from the chair to create a more attractive recruitment offer.

There can be a fine line between safeguarding the peace of others and creating a lack of transparency. To be clear, I am not suggesting that we justify hiding important information from others to be kind or to protect them. Nor do I suggest that a leader's job is to calm everyone down. These motivations can steer a leader toward saviorism, narcissism, and overwork—conflicting with their ability to advance liberation in their setting. Transparency is best practiced when it is in service of freeing up the environment. To evaluate why you want to share information with someone else, assess whether the information is ethical to share and whether you have permission or the right to share it. If you answer in the affirmative, reflect on why you want to share the information: Do you need help with problem-solving? Does the other person need the information to do their work? If the answer is no, then do not share the information. You might realize that you want to vent with someone. Consider whether this feeds into gossip or whether there are other ways to vent that do not include upsetting the peace of others unnecessarily.

Make It Possible for Others to Say No

Finally, allow others to say no more often. I took to including a disclaimer whenever I invited someone to join a committee. In an email, it might go something like this:

> I am inviting you to serve on this committee because I value the skills and experiences that you could bring to this group's work. I also know that you are probably committed to a lot of different activities already. Please feel free to decline this invitation if it is not of interest or does not fit into your schedule at this time. It is more important to me that you have a healthy workload than for you to say yes and then get stressed out. If you decline, I will not think less of you and I will continue to keep you in mind for future opportunities.

For employees from marginalized backgrounds, I also included an acknowledgment of their invisible labor. Faculty and staff responded favorably when I began including this message in my invitations. I probably received more declines this way, but I also built capacity for people to set limits on their time, which countered the culture of overwork.

I have also taken to telling employees that they can use me as their "no" person if they are being pressed into service and cannot say no because they fear reprisal, retaliation, or simply disapproval. For instance, they could say that they consulted with me as the unit leader or as their mentor and that I recommended they decline because of their other commitments. In addition to safeguarding the peace of others, this strategy began to disrupt an oppressive practice of strong-arming less powerful colleagues to do intensive service.

Summary

Liberatory work is rewarding. It can also be challenging to push against oppressive systems. To thrive in work and in life, liberatory leaders require strength and stamina to engage in the long-term work of culture change. Safeguarding our peace allows us to rest and replenish our energy to thrive as individuals and to build cultures of well-being and health with others. Strategies leaders can use to restore mind, body, and spirit include setting boundaries, clearly communicating our values, and engaging in activities that bring rest and joy. We can also spread liberatory culture change by accompanying others in ways that safeguard their peace. If we are fortunate, our colleagues may come to embrace these practices too. It is also possible that we may face resistance or antagonism from those who benefit from oppressive culture. For instance, they may make more demands on our time, may not honor our requests or practices, or may try to provoke us out of our peace. In these cases, the system may be too broken and it may be time to assess your next steps in leadership.

Questions for Reflection and Action

- What cues indicate that it is time for you to focus on safeguarding your peace?
- How does protecting your inner peace give you energy to pursue a liberatory vision?
- What is the most difficult aspect of safeguarding your peace? What is one strategy you can use to do it anyway?
- Whom can you enlist to help support you in safeguarding your peace?
- What strategies can you apply to your calendar to set liberating boundaries for yourself?
- How can you get more rest to safeguard your peace?
- What activities can you engage in to cultivate joy in your daily life?
- Identify someone who appears to effectively safeguard their peace. What lessons can you take from their leadership?
- How might you accompany one of your teammates or colleagues by safeguarding their peace? How might you collectively safeguard each other's peace?

CHAPTER 8

Assessing Your Next Steps in Leadership

I have been fortunate to work with leaders who exemplify principles of liberatory leadership as outlined in this book: critical consciousness raising, accompaniment, and courage. But I have also experienced oppressive environments, including ones created by supervisors who gaslit my colleagues and me; made decisions that solely benefited themselves, including taking credit for other people's work; or squashed creative and collective problem-solving. I will always remember one situation in which my health and well-being took a nosedive. Even then, I could not bring myself to step down because I felt a responsibility to my team. If I could just hang on, then I could buffer people from the toxicity that was generated above me. I also felt a responsibility to show how a unit could function effectively with a woman of color in leadership. A wise person who observed the situation asked me why I stayed. She patiently waited for me to explain my reasons, after which she pointed out that no one should put up with such harmful leadership. Leaving on my own terms could demonstrate to others that they too did not have to put up with oppression now or in the future. Living my values by leaving could model courageous action for others. It took me several months to finally announce my departure, but that experience solidified for me the importance of remaining true to my values at work. Leaving can be the most liberating action we can take, for ourselves and for others.

Oppressive leadership is just one situation that may motivate you to evaluate your next steps. It may also be the case that exciting new opportunities to engage in the work of liberation will come your way. If you are fortunate, there will come a point when you have learned what you set out to learn, cocreated programs and a new way of working, and set up others for successful leadership. Now it's time for you to sow the seeds of liberatory leadership doing something else. In these situations, you may feel ready to seek out a new challenge that aligns with your values. Often, those new opportunities do not arise until we make a choice to leave or to at least say to ourselves, "I'm ready for what's next." Whether you are content or dissatisfied with your current role, considering your next steps is made easier when you reflect on the past and current motivations that have led you to the present time. It is also wise to examine fears, experiences, or beliefs that may be holding you back from your next liberating step. In this chapter, I offer guidance to ascertain when and how to move on from a leadership position, even if it is a fulfilling one, to seek greater freedom for yourself and for others.

Before I continue, it is important to acknowledge that simply walking away from an oppressive situation is not possible for everyone. A host of factors affect the ease with which you can leave and the alternatives that may be acceptable to you. These include financial considerations, ties to the community and culture, local kin and friendship networks, caregiving responsibilities, school options for children, partner employment, access to health insurance, and immigration status, to name a few. Nevertheless, it is worth examining the scripts that you have learned from life experiences, loved ones, and other sources that may be playing an outsize role in deliberations. For instance, in my own life, an unexamined and unhealthy attachment to stability and predictability held me back from a liberating future for myself and my family. This desire made some sense given my own family history. I come from a long line of so-called unskilled laborers on both sides of my family whose schedules and pay were decided by employers who weren't always equity minded. My parents drilled into me that one of the most important goals of a college education was to land a good-paying, stable job; having any control over my work would be a bonus. This socialization played a big role in my decision to try to become a professor with tenure. With time and experience, I came to learn that this attraction to stability and my efforts to play it safe could also serve as an obstacle to liberating possibilities.

The lesson here is that there may be good reasons for you to choose to stay put. At the same time, be curious in case some of the reasons no longer apply. Your desire to cocreate liberatory working environments can sit alongside other dearly held values and obligations. Taking a cue from the critical consciousness-raising work at the outset of this book, let's examine why you are where you are at this moment.

Reexamine Your Values

You may have used a liberatory mission to guide your entry into the role you currently hold. Or you may have filled your current role for a variety of other reasons: salary and benefits, no one else wanted to do it, or it just seemed like the right next step. Regardless of the reasons you ended up here, now is a great time to examine how you are resisting oppression and embracing a liberatory mindset.

Consider identifying the metrics or observable outcomes that can show that you are doing the work of liberation. These metrics can help you stay on course, know when it's time to leave, and discern new opportunities to pursue. The following questions are ideal to ask when you start a new position, but they can be used any time to assess the extent to which you have been able to practice your liberatory aspirations:

What do you hope to learn in this role? From a liberatory leadership perspective, your list might include greater knowledge and skills in critical self-awareness, accompaniment and solidarity, and courageous action. How will you go about learning or deepening these skills?

What new reality do you wish to cocreate with your colleagues? Given your institutional context, perhaps there are mission-aligned programs, curricula, or policies that need to be implemented to achieve shared goals.

How do you want to empower others for sustained liberation? We all have examples of initiatives and programs that faded away or were unceremoniously discontinued upon the departure of the leader who championed them. You will likely not hold your leadership position forever, so think about your legacy.

Reconnecting with why you do what you do can prevent stagnation and recharge your batteries. This kind of reflection may also result in the realization that it's time to consider other paths.

Reflecting on the Obstacles That Hold Us Back

No matter the reason for seeking new opportunities, leaders can benefit from reflection to ensure they continue to act from a place of freedom and wholeness. Without this reflection, leaders risk choosing a new role that limits the liberatory impact they can have, and they might even contribute to continued oppression for themselves and others. This is what a colleague of mine learned in her quest for a job in which she could thrive. "Brenda" was a woman of the global majority who was deeply committed to accompanying and supporting students from marginalized communities. Students appreciated her sense of care, and she witnessed many go into rewarding careers. Brenda was well respected by her peers and had been promoted several times. Eventually a new supervisor was hired. He began taking credit for Brenda's and her colleagues' work. He neglected to invite them to important meetings that would make sense for them to attend, and he undermined Brenda by asking her supervisees to come directly to him with questions. Brenda initially tried to find ways to work with this new boss, but the stress took a toll on her health. She shared her concerns with trusted others and with existing institutional offices designed to support employees, but nothing changed. Brenda realized it was time to leave. Out of desperation to get out as quickly as possible, she began applying for every opening for which she was qualified. When trusted confidants reflected back to her the most rewarding part of her job—helping students bring their authentic selves to their studies and build skills in their chosen fields—she realized it was best to be more selective so that she did not reproduce her current experience. Although this realization slowed her exit, it resulted in a better long-term job outcome. Brenda's motivation may have begun with an urge to escape an increasingly oppressive situation, but her reconnection with her purpose ensured that she landed in a situation in which she could flourish.

This example may strike a nerve with some readers who are intimately familiar with the impact of oppressive leadership. My point is not to depress but to be realistic. There will be times when we find ourselves in situations that were not what we initially thought. Leaders or institutional changes may also shift the culture in oppressive ways. Yet we can learn to resist oppression and keep thriving by reading the reality of the situation against the backdrop of our values and motivations. In this case, Brenda was able to recognize that the work was inspiring but that her supervisor and institutional culture were the problems. She learned that she needed to leave to preserve her health and continue her liberatory work. She also learned how to set boundaries to persist in her valued work while she sought out other opportunities. And she learned to pay close attention to her values as she interviewed. These were valuable insights for Brenda, and they can also aid the rest of us who want to address the reality of oppression in the academic workplace.

In addition to reflecting on your motivations, it is wise to search for the "unfreedoms" that may be holding you back from making liberatory changes for yourself. It's nearly impossible to be perfectly free from pessimistic mindsets, self-limiting beliefs, or oppressive forces, but we can try to be "free enough." Ignacio Martín-Baró, Ignacio Ellacuría, and their colleagues at the Universidad Centroamericana, as part of their pastoral development as Jesuits, had many years of training in the art of discernment, including how to weigh the various attachments that might prevent them from having enough inner freedom to act. Let's explore some of the obstacles that prevent us from taking healthy risks and following new liberating paths.

Unexamined Fears

As a first-generation college student, I was rewarded for planning and researching my next steps. Academia is filled with planners like me. Planning helped us finish our degrees, go on the job market, and complete projects. Yet this tendency to plan can get in the way of freedom. When we let our fear of losing control get the better of us, we may refrain from exploring new opportunities that seem risky or that do not fit into an established path. I have worked with many people who could not allow themselves to consider new projects or roles because they were afraid of the unknown. They feared making a mistake they would regret later. Known as "regret aversion" by behavioral economists, this type of emotional forecasting can block us from taking a risk. We think we are not making a choice. In reality, we choose the status quo, even if it's contributing to our own oppression.

Fear also comes in the form of anticipated loss. We have all witnessed people who overstayed their welcomes because they apparently did not want to lose a large salary, honorific titles, or power and control. Of course, money, honors, and authority can be used in ways that support liberation for ourselves, our families, and colleagues. Yet an unhealthy fear of losing these things can also get in the way of making changes that would be even more liberatory. If one of your obstacles has to do with loss of money, status, or power, it's time to review your personal mission and consider how strongly the fear of loss is playing into your decisions relative to other aspects of your mission.

And finally, fear can show up in your beliefs about yourself. When we are reluctant to seek out new opportunities because we think we are not good enough, we've fallen prey to imposter syndrome. This phrase was coined by psychologists Pauline Clance and Suzanne Imes in 1978 to describe self-doubt about one's abilities and the fear of being found out as a fraud. Initially, it was thought that the way to overcome these irrational beliefs was for individuals to build confidence. I embrace how inclusive leadership experts Ruchika Tulshyan and Jodi-Ann Burney (2021) turn this concept on its head in their article "Stop Telling Women They Have Imposter Syndrome." Rather than viewing feelings of imposterism as a personal defect, these authors argue that systems of oppression have made those who are marginalized or excluded feel like imposters to keep them in their places. With microaggressions and other exclusionary behaviors, status quo gatekeepers tell others that they are not good enough. The next time you think you will be "found out" if you spread your wings, remember that this voice is the result of many years of messaging designed to hold us back from a liberated future.

An antidote to these fears—the fear of the unknown, fear of loss, and fear that we're not good enough—is asking questions. Start with yourself and consider your fears: What are you afraid will happen, and where is this belief coming from? What information do you need to evaluate the extent to which the feared outcome is likely? I recall waiting a long time before I applied to be a fellow in my professional organization because I thought I needed just the right qualifications or else the committee would deny my application and think I wasted their time. Shortly after I achieved fellow status, a male colleague asked me to write a letter of support for his application. He had a solid CV, but it was not as extensive as mine. If I had asked myself, "Is it really true that I have to wait until I have the perfect CV?" or, "What is the perfect CV in the first place?" or even, "What's so bad about being turned down for not having all the experience yet?" I might have applied at an earlier stage of my career.

Rely on your community as well. Talk to an executive coach, trusted confidants, loved ones, and colleagues, all of whom may have a more objective view of your capabilities and the risks involved. I have also found that networking in person and virtually (e.g., on LinkedIn) is essential to building courage and knowledge. Not only have I met interesting colleagues and collaborators who inspire me with their courage, but through their eyes, I have learned that I also bring unique skills and experiences to the table.

Oppressive Leadership

Oppressive leadership behaviors can also get in the way of our liberation path. I recall one situation in which I was convinced that I could tolerate and work around a difficult leader because we were making progress on initiatives that were meaningful to me. I believed that if I changed my approach, maybe things would change. It took some time for me to realize that the leader was the problem. It was not "wrong" for me to do some introspection first; self-reflection and humility are certainly required of people engaged in liberation praxis. But sometimes looking within results in excessive persistence that can get in the way of liberating action. If you feel like you have to become a different person to survive, it may be time to realize that oppressive leadership is holding you back.

Also observe leaders who have a misalignment between their words and actions. For instance, I have witnessed leaders who say they value their team but then put them down in closed-door meetings with other leaders or undermine them and their agency by telling them what to do and how to do it. If you find yourself in this situation, even if others do not believe the leader, the energy you spend managing the misinformation can get in the way of your own leadership.

A more insidious behavior pattern is gaslighting, a form of manipulation in which the leader attempts to control another person by questioning their experience or withholding information. This behavior sows confusion and self-doubt in the target person and increases their dependence on the only "true" source of valid information: the leader. In one unit in which gaslighting was known to be the norm, I witnessed high turnover rates. Few felt safe enough to disclose why they left. Almost everyone knew about what it was like to work with this leader, but this person was permitted to remain in office. How telling this was of the institutional culture!

There may be a whole host of reasons why some leaders persist in engaging in these oppressive tactics, including insecurity, ego, and pressure from above. The reality is that the motivations don't really matter; the behaviors contribute to toxic and oppressive environments regardless. Yet there is one situation where it might be wise to consider a leader's motive more closely: when it appears that the leader is forcing you out. Many leaders, especially those who have risen up the faculty ranks, have not been trained to appreciate and deliver progressive feedback to develop their teams. In the absence of this basic leadership development training, leaders dial up the pressure with the goal of coaxing individuals to leave, a tactic called "quiet firing" (Ruvio and Morgeson, 2022). Exclusionary tactics include dropping people from committees or assignments, neglecting to invite them to important meetings, or assigning more work without providing commensurate compensation, time, or resources to accomplish the task. In my experience, these tactics are often used to push out people with marginalized identities and others who threaten the status quo by advancing liberatory agendas. When the employee resigns, the institution reports that the person decided to leave of their own accord. This is especially difficult to make sense of when institutions have mission statements that stress social justice and inclusion.

If you notice any of these oppressive leadership behaviors in your workplace, consider checking in with trusted colleagues and allies to learn how they are experiencing the situation. Connecting with colleagues may reveal that the leader is open to learning and doing better. With your colleagues, you may be able to discern who is the most appropriate person to "manage up" or coach the leader about the impact of their behavior and how they can correct it. Yet in environments with prolonged oppressive leadership or that are not psychologically safe, providing feedback may not be safe.

Still, checking in with colleagues or confidants can shed light on reality. A colleague of mine persisted a little longer than she needed to in one role because she neglected to talk to colleagues about the situation. She internalized the problem and thought it was her own to solve. Once she talked to others, she realized that her experiences were not isolated incidents and they were not merely the result of bad chemistry between her and the leader. She and her colleagues had a shared experience with a common denominator—an insecure and retaliatory leader. Reading reality for what it was freed up the team to choose next steps. One left the unit, one set out to develop skills to prepare for a move, and another remained and set healthier limits.

Reading reality may also mean that you realize you have become a target of discrimination or harassment. If that is the case, Kim Scott (2021) offers several suggestions to disentangle yourself from this form of workplace violence. She recommends documenting the facts and building solidarity, as well as making choices about whether to make a report to HR, take legal action, or share your experience publicly.

Feeling (Too) Responsible

Most people would agree that leaders should have a healthy dose of responsibility, otherwise nothing would get done. At the same time, feeling too much responsibility may be a sign of an oppressive system. While leaders may feel a responsibility to stay, it may make more sense to leave. This feeling of responsibility can be particularly strong among tokenized leaders with marginalized identities who recognize what their leadership represents to others. Leaders who are saddled with the work of institutional culture change may also feel this keenly. We might fear that our departures will slow or halt much-needed culture change. As the "only" or "first" in several positions, I know the weight of this responsibility. While it may initially come from a place of good intentions, taking on too much responsibility for change can become an obstacle to liberating action. If there were more people of color, more LGBTQ+ people, or more people with disabilities in leadership, then the departure of one leader would not feel like the end of the world. With very few leaders from marginalized groups, any departure is a cause for hand-wringing. If part of your felt sense of responsibility comes from the institution overburdening you, it's time to free yourself from thinking that this is your problem. Stop taking responsibility for work that is not yours to do.

Looking back on the opening story for this chapter, I recognize that staying in a toxic situation because I felt responsible for the well-being of others was a bit self-serving; I fell into the leadership trap of feeling like I had the power to protect others. All the people I worked with were adults who could make their own decisions. In that situation, staying would have sent the message that it was totally acceptable to put up with oppressive leadership even if it meant sacrificing one's well-being. My colleague helped me realize that making a choice that was healthy for me could be freeing for others. When we sacrifice our health and freedom in order to permit oppression to continue, we are not doing the work of liberation. We are acquiescing to the status quo.

Burnout and Exhaustion

Resentment, fatigue, and burnout can all serve as obstacles to our ability to carry out liberating change. Rebecca Pope-Ruark (2022) adopts a definition of workplace burnout that includes extreme exhaustion, disaffection and cynicism, and perceived ineffectiveness. Workplace burnout and other forms of stress-induced exhaustion can sap the energy and hope that are needed for forward-looking reflection. Therefore, it is wise to refrain from making big career decisions during times of depletion. Take care of yourself first. Pope-Ruark's suggestions include cutting out essential and nonessential activities so you can let go of unreasonable expectations and free yourself to reconnect with your deepest purpose. Caring for yourself might also include talking to a therapist, especially if you are experiencing a loss of interest in activities that you once found enjoyable, a depressed mood more days than not, anxiety, or other symptoms that are interfering with your ability to function in everyday life.

Once you are revitalized *enough*, it may be useful to pause and examine your road to burnout. How much of your experience was due to oppressive features of your workplace like a culture of overwork; racist, sexist, and ableist practices and policies at your institution or in your discipline; or internalized oppressive expectations? To what extent do you have the agency and support to resist these oppressive forces? It can be freeing to realize that we have more agency than we may have initially thought. For instance, just because you said yes to a thankless and exhausting leadership role no one else wanted does not mean that you are stuck with it forever. Short of leaving this role, there may be ways to put a time limit on your leadership, delegate portions of the work, or alter the scope of the work. As long as you continue to feel spent and exhausted, it is difficult to envision *un otro mundo posible* (an other possible world). Taking the time to recover can free up your cognitive and emotional resources to assess your next steps on a liberating path.

When You Can't or Don't Want to Leave

As noted earlier, there may be good reasons you cannot consider a departure right now. It may be a sound decision to stay put. Yet you can still maintain your peace and live your liberatory values through developing allies and coconspirators, securing projects that are meaningful to you, or engaging in meaningful professional development or working with a coach. Find outlets for liberation work outside of your employment, including through community and social service organizations.

Other readers who are in a position to consider a change might dismiss the need to think about next steps because they are satisfied with where they are. It is still a good practice to periodically reflect on your current situation and where you are headed so you are prepared when opportunity strikes. This is a great time to dig deeper into your personal liberatory mission using the questions in the first part of this chapter. You can also examine what type of work you would love to pursue next. Rather than titles that connote power, what types of liberatory activities and initiatives do you enjoy now that you can pursue in a future role? What other projects or ways of working would you like to learn about, and how can you build the skills and knowledge to prepare for when this opportunity presents itself later? It's also a great time to consider whether your desire to stay put comes from a place of complacency and comfort with what is known. As Margaret Silf (2007, 81) writes, "Often the choice lies between the good and the better. The good can sometimes be the enemy of the better. To choose well is to choose the better." If we never examine the question, "What is the better?" we may find ourselves stuck in merely good situations, limiting our own liberatory potential and that of others.

Planning Your Exit

Once you realize that the time has come to move on, do your research about the type of work you feel called to do. If you have your eyes on a particular role or institution, search for articles in the *Chronicle of Higher Education, Inside Higher Ed*, and other outlets to learn about the institution's initiatives, culture, and challenges. Check in with colleagues who have worked at the institution and with its leaders to learn more about the culture, climate, and valued priorities. How did these leaders make decisions about personnel, curriculum, fundraising, and strategic direction? Who is on their leadership team? To what extent are leaders living a mission that is aligned with your values to lead from a liberatory stance?

Search firms can be excellent sources of information as well. Consultants can clue you in to the challenges and opportunities for a given opening, and they can help you more accurately appraise your readiness. A conversation can also help you determine the extent to which this position would allow you to live out your personal mission. Ask them pointed questions about why they reached out to you. Why are your skills and experiences attractive? Why are you a good candidate for this role? Why did the incumbent depart? These same questions are useful to consider when you are invited to interview and when an offer is extended. In addition to researching the financial health of the organization, think about the budgetary and personnel resources required to support the liberating action you will lead. Will these resources be available to you? How might other leaders share or support your liberatory vision?

When it comes time to depart, put some thought into announcing your exit in a way that promotes healing and freedom for others. As an act of accompaniment, it is ideal if you can be the one to break the news to your team and closest colleagues. Even if your supervisor wishes to be the first to announce the news, there are ways to accompany others. For instance, you might personally reach out to those who are most vulnerable or colleagues with whom you collaborated most closely. In emails, on social media, or in remarks at a farewell gathering, celebrate the liberatory work you have done together. Consider also what your team may need to be successful in continuing liberatory work. Support their agency and hope by reminding them that they have the mindset, the team, and the skills to continue this work. Put them in touch with other like-minded folks, including sponsors and mentors who advance liberatory perspectives. Seed continued liberation with your parting words and actions.

Keep in mind that many people will try to read between the lines when your departure is announced. As human beings, we cannot help but be curious, especially when the news is a surprise. When I departed from one of my leadership positions, I had a mix of responses, including one person who offered to protest on my behalf. They needed reassurance that I was not fired or forced out; I chose to leave. While I was flattered by their willingness to advocate for me, this example highlights that people will search for meaning in your departure. Depending on circumstances (e.g., nondisclosure agreements), you may wish to tell more of the truth than is typical in these announcements. There may be reasons to reveal injustice if there is a chance that the truth can serve a liberatory purpose. For example, your public truth telling might foster a growing critical consciousness among faculty and staff, or solidarity with others facing similar oppression. Two recent examples offer inspiration. In February 2023, Ruth Simmons offered a great example of truth telling in her announcement that she was resigning as president of Prairie View A&M University. And in January 2024, Claudine Gay named racism, sexism, and fear as factors that led to her resignation as president of Harvard University. Although these statements did not change the situation, these courageous leaders put the institutions and the public on notice about the oppressive realities at play. They also empowered other leaders by providing powerful models of integrity.

Mutual *Acompañamiento y Empoderamiento*

As we disentangle ourselves from oppressive beliefs and environments, we will find ourselves in what Chicana poet, activist, and author Gloria Anzaldúa ([1987] 2012, 42) refers to as *los intersticios*. The time in between choosing to leave and actually leaving is one of these interstitial or liminal spaces that can elicit a range of emotions: relief and grief, excitement and guilt, and everything in between. When I realized that I needed to depart from one of my leadership roles, I felt guilt and regret about how my career choice affected my family. Perhaps it would have been smoother for them if I had not taken the job in the first place. I felt sadness about letting some people down for not sticking it out, especially untenured colleagues who had told me that my approach inspired them. I felt anger that other leaders were not creating the conditions in which we could thrive. At the same time, I was excited about my future. A jumble of emotions, to be sure! As I spoke with loved ones, colleagues, and allies, I realized that some of my feelings were coming from a place of fear, and others were to be expected considering the circumstances. Find people who can accompany you on these emotional ups and downs by validating your experience as real and helping you to make sense of *los intersticios*. Find people who can be sources of *empoderamiento* (empowerment).

The lessons of El Salvador can also help us welcome *acompañamiento*. Recall that accompaniment is not unidirectional; leaders also need to be accompanied. The Comunidades Eclesiales de Base accompanied leaders, offering encouragement and support during their departures and transitions. This was most evident when thousands of people risked their lives to attend funerals and memorial services for Archbishop Óscar Arnulfo

Romero, the Jesuit martyrs of the Universidad Centroamericana, and others in the midst of violent repression. This mutual accompaniment continues today. Comunidades Eclesiales de Base remember these leaders with memorials, *testimonio*, and images hanging in their community centers. In turn, the memories of these leaders fuel continued liberating action.

In the United States, leadership departures are not as fraught as the martyrdom experienced in El Salvador and other parts of the world. For the most part, we have the time and the safety to offer and receive accompaniment as we say goodbye. People who valued your leadership will feel loss, fear about the future, and happiness for you. An email of support, a cup of coffee, or a listening ear might be ways they would like to show their solidarity and gratitude. For many of us, being on the receiving end of such accompaniment might feel uncomfortable; we do not have many examples of leaders accepting accompaniment. Learning to accept support is just another opportunity to practice mutual accompaniment and empowerment. If it is reasonable, offer to stay in touch. What could be perceived as an end may be an opportunity to continue the relationship in a new way.

Also be prepared for people who are not able or willing to accompany you. These colleagues might center their own feelings of loss, or they might have internalized institutional loyalty at all costs. I experienced this kind of reaction on two separate occasions when I departed for another institution. The first time it happened, I felt extremely guilty because the senior faculty told me, an untenured assistant professor, that it was like I was leaving "the family." The second instance occurred after I had advanced to full professor. Most of my colleagues were happy that I had an opportunity that was aligned with my values. But one colleague implied that I was not loyal in seeking an opportunity elsewhere. People who attempt to make others feel guilty have work to do to free themselves from their own insecurities and internalized oppression. They relied on you far more than they should have. Ideally, along with sadness about your leaving, colleagues will be excited about your new opportunities.

Finally, accept gratitude. In a last meeting with one of my teams, I tried to reassure them that they would not feel my departure. They had all the tools they needed to continue their important work individually and as the cohesive team they were. I had every confidence in them. One member of the team interrupted me to say that the team would not have been able to function the way it did without my example of leadership. In my effort to ensure they felt at peace with their future, I had not made the space for them to share back their gratitude for my leadership. In protecting myself from the sadness of leaving, I was preventing everyone, including myself, from being able to move on. It was a great example of solidarity and accompaniment. This exchange was also a good reminder for me that accompaniment is not unidirectional. In that moment, we needed to accompany each other for mutual liberation.

Summary

Assessment of your next steps in leadership does not need to wait until you are ready to leave an oppressive workplace. Reexamining unspoken fears, your encounters with oppressive leadership, and your hopes for a thriving culture can help you realize when it is time to explore other, more liberating options. A liberatory mindset can also guide how you accompany others so they can continue cocreating *un otro mundo posible* in academia.

Questions for Reflection and Action

- What is it about your current role that continues to be aligned with your personal mission? What is it about your current role that is no longer aligned with your mission?
- Imagine if you remained in your current position for one more year (or one more month or five more years). How do your reactions inform your choice to continue in this role?
- What are the what-ifs that hold you back from exploring new opportunities?
- If you are experiencing oppressive or toxic leadership, what are the consequences of staying? Of leaving?
- What is "the good" versus "the better" choice in front of you? How do these choices support your liberatory values?
- Whom can you reach out to when you find yourself in *los intersticios*?
- How can you accompany your team as you depart? How can you welcome their accompaniment?

CHAPTER 9

Parting Thoughts

Liberation is a practice. As a practice, it requires ongoing reflection and action in community with others. This is the model given to us by the Jesuits of the Universidad Centroamericano, the Comunidades Eclesiales de Base, and countless others in El Salvador and other parts of the world who have worked and continue to work toward a liberated future. Applied to the academic workplace, leadership centered on liberation, when practiced by more than just one person, can undo harmful policies and norms that have oppressed employees, students, and communities since the beginning. I have many hopes for readers of this book. I hope it provides a rationale for leaders who are just recognizing that an aim of leadership is to free up oppressive systems. I hope this book serves as validation for leaders who have already been leading toward liberation but did not have the words to describe their path. And I hope that this book gives courage to people who feel lonely, isolated, or depleted but believe that something else is possible. Each of us can contribute to healthier environments in which everyone can be free to bring their gifts and talents to address challenges we face as a society.

I have no illusions about how challenging this work can be. While it is freeing to remind myself that none of us can do this on our own or even complete this work in our lifetimes, it can still be demoralizing when we do not immediately see the fruits of our labor. I am writing this closing section during a volatile time in society and in higher education in the United States. In summer 2023, the Supreme Court of the United States, by a six-to-three vote, overturned affirmative action in college admissions. In addition, lawmakers in a number of US states have outlawed programs and offices that support broader access to higher education, enhance student belongingness, and ensure a workforce that is skilled enough to engage with diverse constituents. Politicians are also questioning the value of certain scholarly disciplines and stacking university boards with members who are antagonistic toward anything that smacks of diversity, equity, and inclusion (DEI). They are also pitting marginalized and excluded groups against each other under the guise of promoting safety and civil discourse on campus. In turn, university leaders are being vilified and ousted for advancing social justice. This is a problem faced not only by colleges and universities; private companies are also being sued and threatened with lawsuits for attempting to level the playing field and ensure they have diverse talent.

Observations by Sharon Stein, Ariana González Stokas, Robin D. G. Kelley, and others that we cannot DEI our way out of oppression were prescient. Indeed, systems of oppression can be slippery; language and laws can be used to appeal to fairness and freedom when, in fact, they purposefully evade and obscure the reality of racism, sexism, and other harmful systems that result in marginalization, exclusion, devaluing, silencing, and violence. Case in point are comments made by senior white male faculty members who claimed that I, a woman of color leader, was not being inclusive as I moved forward with institutional priorities of inclusion, complaints that triggered a review of my leadership. I sustained the attempt to discredit my effective leadership but the time and energy my team and I spent on conducting this review could have been used more productively.

How can we keep going in the face of oppression? There were moments while writing this book when I wondered, "What's the point of encouraging people to lead differently if it might not result in change; if it will result in punishment?" and, "Am I being unrealistic or even doing harm by suggesting we try to do things differently?" Two concepts have helped me get unstuck from this oppressive self-talk and pessimistic rumination: *un otro mundo posible* (an other possible world) and dreamstorming. Taking a cue from the Jesuits, Archbishop Óscar Arnulfo Romero, the Comunidades Eclesiales de Base, and other liberation practitioners, *un otro mundo posible* articulates a strong faith in a liberated future that is better than the current reality (Gandolfo and Potter, 2022); a reality in which everyone can be fully human (Freire, [1970] 2000). From this perspective, I am confident that oppressive academic culture is not the only possible reality.

Once we use our imaginations to envision a new reality, we can take steps to bring it about. We can engage in this imaginative envisioning through what psychologist Jennifer Gómez calls dreamstorming (Gómez, 2023a, 2023b). Dreamstorming is "the process of envisioning liberation, as well as the paths it would take to create and inhabit a world of true freedom" (Gómez, 2023a, 134). Dreamstorming in higher education can orient "our vision to fundamentally eradicating the interlocking systems of oppression that uphold violence and oppression in higher education and society" (Gómez, 2023b).

Imagining *un otro mundo posible* through dreamstorming can produce ideas to reinvent higher education as a catalyst of liberating societal change. This reinvention is already happening. Kelley (2016) describes several movements of scholars who are questioning how universities maintain power and reinforce the status quo of society. He provides an example in the Mississippi Freedom Schools, which were created by the Student Nonviolent Coordinating Committee during the 1964 Freedom Summer. These schools were intended to help students challenge the unquestioned assumptions of society, to read reality for what it was, and to imagine alternatives. Another contemporary example is described by Abigail Boggs and colleagues (2019), who advocate for abolitionist university studies, a scholarly area that counters the accumulative and extractive properties of American higher education. An abolitionist approach includes reading and critiquing the reality that universities are sites of oppression, and using the imagination to build what might seem to be the impossible. Abolitionist universities choose to engage in actions that upend norms of accumulation, extraction, and oppression. Other dreamstormed examples of possible higher education futures are offered by reparations (González Stokas, 2023), decolonial (Stein, 2022), and critical university studies scholars (Boggs and Mitchell, 2018). By engaging in a scholarship of questioning and love, perhaps we too can dream up a different way of engaging in the educational enterprise.

Dreamstorming *un otro mundo posible* is made possible by applying many of the skills and practices described in this book: reading personal and institutional realities with a liberatory lens, accompanying others and being transformed by our communities, risking courageous action, creating opportunities for others to lead, safeguarding our peace so we have the room to dream, and moving on to other opportunities. In my own work, I have observed that my supervisors, colleagues, students, and I have been able to dream big and develop the most creative solutions when we collectively engage in these elements of liberation praxis. Because we approached our work differently, we developed novel solutions to seemingly impossible challenges. We had the capacity to dream and a renewed energy to address complex problems concerning curriculum, research and scholarly activity, budget and personnel, student, community, and fundraising challenges.

We all benefit when we have a critical mass of leaders who have the capacity to dreamstorm a liberating future into reality. Will you join us?

ACKNOWLEDGMENTS

Thank you, Reader, for taking action to liberate higher education from oppression. Your efforts do not go unnoticed! And yet, collective action for liberation is not possible without recognizing that much of the land upon which we live and work is unceded and stolen Indigenous land. The land on which this book was written is the unceded ancestral and contemporary homeland of the Spokane Tribe of Indians. I honor the Indigenous stewards of this land, past and present, and I express gratitude for the ways in which this land supported me while I wrote this book. I recognize my responsibility as a beneficiary of colonization to confront its ongoing harms, and I encourage readers of this book to do the same.

A book about liberation praxis is also not possible without community. And I am so grateful for the *acompañamiento* of my community! A big thank-you to my executive coach Tarry Paylor, who took to saying, "That needs to go in your book," whenever I told her one of my stories. I finally had to ask her if she meant a metaphorical book or a real one (she meant the latter). I wouldn't have set out to write this book if not for her liberating observation that these stories could do more good if they were shared with others.

Thank you to all the early readers who provided feedback on the book proposal and chapter drafts: Mirjeta Beqiri, Cassy Dame-Griffe, Yoli Gallardo, Liz O'Donnell Gandolfo, Jennifer Gómez, Jennifer Hart, Robin(ette) Kelley, Dorine Lawrence-Hughes, Jacqueline McCormick, Dawn Medley, Julia Chinyere Oparah, Tarry Paylor, Jonathan Rossing, Monica Ulibarri, Deborah Uman, Etta Ward, and Lee Wurm. Your generosity of spirit, enthusiasm, and solidarity mattered greatly, especially when the writing process dredged up feelings and experiences I had not previously processed.

To the anonymous reviewers, thank you for your thoughtful and encouraging feedback, which strengthened my conviction about why this book needed to be written. I am also appreciative of the Johns Hopkins editorial team for helping this book come to fruition. Special thanks to editor Greg Britton, whose curiosity motivated me during the proposal stage and whose vision, support, and good humor sustained me during the writing and publication process.

I am grateful for the leaders who created conditions of thriving for me to grow into my leadership philosophy, including Nancy Cantor, John Darley, Joe Dunbar, Dan O'Leary, and Keith Whitfield. Much appreciation also goes to the amazing leaders with whom I worked while writing this book, including the "COVID Deans" group from the Association of Jesuit Colleges and Universities: Heidi Bostic, Bonnie Gunzenhauser, Michelle Maldonado, and Daniel Press; the Gonzaga University Council of Deans led by provost Deena González; Tara McAloon; Kecia Thomas; and the HERS Bryn Mawr 2017 cohort. I also express gratitude for my students and coaching clients, who continue to inspire me with their questions, observations, and courageous leadership. They show that another world is possible and needed in academia.

I first learned about the Jesuits of the Universidad Centroamericana from Fr. Bernie Owens when I saw a poster in his office at Manresa Jesuit Retreat House in Bloomfield Hills, MI. Thank you, Fr. Bernie, for serving as an *animador* of discernment. And thanks to other Jesuits who walked with me and deepened my appreciation of being "free enough" to pursue the greater good through the Spiritual Exercises of St. Ignatius of Loyola: Fr. J.K. Adams, Fr. Leo Cachat, Fr. Phil Cooke, Fr. Peter Etzel, Fr. Walt Farrell, Fr. Peter Fennessy, Fr. Tom Lamanna, Fr. Dan Nevares, Fr. Jim Serrick, and Fr. Gilbert Sunghera. I have also been fortunate to know and learn from a number of "Jesuettes," women who embodied the Ignatian way of freedom: my first spiritual director, Barbara Steele (who coined the term Jesuette); Artemae Anderson; Beth Barsotti; Lauren Hackman-Brooks; Gabrielle Lee; Jeanne Lord; Diane Neville; Rita Amberg Waldref; and Michelle Wheatley. Thank you for modeling the way with grace and strength. *Ad Majorem Dei Gloriam.*

I am grateful also for the witness and teaching of members of the Comunidades Eclesiales de Base whom I was fortunate to meet during my first trip to the Bajo Lempa region in the department of Usulután, El Salvador, in 2023, especially José Salvador "Chamba" Ruiz, Rossy Iraheta Marinero, and Maria Tomasa "Tomi" Membreno. *Mil gracias por su testimonio y su profunda hospitalidad.* A huge thank-you to Rita Amberg Waldref, George Waldref, and Cristy Saint for their friendship and for building a strong and lasting relationship with these communities, characterized by solidarity, *acompañamiento*, and collective liberation.

I thank my sister, Susan, who showed unwavering loyalty and confidence in my abilities as I navigated difficult situations during the writing of this book. Everyone should have a ferocious cheerleader like you! Deep gratitude and love to my mom and dad, Luisa (Louise) Tieso y Hernández and Marcelino (Lino) Caño y Neira, for their sacrifices, fortitude, and love, which made everything possible for me. And I send appreciation to all my ancestors. Though the details of their lives may be lost, their resistance lives on.

Thank you, Joseph. Your love and early read of reality have helped me take risks I would not have taken on my own. I hope you see this book as permission to break some rules and create new ones! And Lee, your steadfast support and love boggle the mind. It can't be easy putting up with my nonstop questions and wonderings. I am grateful to have you in my life.

REFERENCES

Ahmed, Sara. 2021. *Complaint!* Durham, NC: Duke University Press.

American Association of Colleges and Universities. 2020. "Even Before the Pandemic, Many Faculty Faced Food Insecurity, Housing Insecurity, or Homelessness." November 1, 2020. https://www.aacu.org/liberaleducation/articles/even-before-the-pandemic-many-faculty-faced-food-insecurity-housing-insecurity-or-homelessness.

Anzaldúa, Gloria Evangelina. (1987) 2012. *Borderlands/La Frontera: The New Mestiza.* 25th anniversary 4th ed. San Francisco: Aunt Lute Books.

Association of Governing Boards of Universities and Colleges. 2021. *Policies, Practices, and Composition of Governing Boards of Colleges, Universities, and Institutionally Related Foundations.* Washington, DC: Association of Governing Boards of Universities and Colleges.

Barshay, Jill. 2022. "PROOF POINTS: 861 Colleges and 9,499 Campuses Have Closed Down Since 2004." Hechinger Report, November 21, 2022. https://hechingerreport.org/proof-points-861-colleges-and-9499-campuses-have-closed-down-since-2004/.

Becker-Blease, Kathryn A. 2017. "As the World Becomes Trauma-Informed, Work to Do." *Journal of Trauma and Dissociation* 18 (2): 131–138. https://doi.org/10.1080/15299732.2017.1253401.

Boggs, Abigail, Eli Meyerhoff, Nick Mitchell, and Zach Schwartz-Weinstein. 2019. "Abolitionist University Studies: An Invitation." *Abolition Journal*, August 28, 2019. https://abolitionjournal.org/abolitionist-university-studies-an-invitation/.

Boggs, Abigail, and Nick Mitchell. 2018. "Critical University Studies and the Crisis Consensus." *Feminist Studies* 44 (2): 432–463. https://doi.org/10.1353/fem.2018.0028.

Bonilla-Silva, Eduardo. 2017. "What We Were, What We Are, and What We Should Be: The Racial Problem of American Sociology." *Social Problems* 64 (2): 179–187. https://doi.org/10.1093/socpro/spx006.

Bourgeault, Ivy, Janet Mantler, and Nicole Power. 2021. "Mental Health in Academia: The Challenges Faculty Face Predate the Pandemic and Require Systemic Solutions." *Academic Matters*, Fall 2021. https://academicmatters.ca/mental-health-in-academia-the-challenges-faculty-face-predate-the-pandemic-and-require-systemic-solutions/.

Brown, Laura S. 2021. "Institutional Cowardice: A Powerful, Often Invisible Manifestation of Institutional Betrayal." *Journal of Trauma and Dissociation* 22 (3): 241–248. https://doi.org/10.1080/15299732.2020.1801307.

Bryant-Davis, Thema, and Lillian Comas-Díaz, eds. 2016. *Womanist and Mujerista Psychologies: Voices of Fire, Acts of Courage*. Washington, DC: American Psychological Association.

Caño, Annmarie. 2023. "A Mistake to Avoid in Leadership Searches." *Inside Higher Ed*, November 7, 2023. https://www.insidehighered.com/opinion/career-advice/2023/11/07/best-job-candidate-isnt-just-someone-who-did-it-opinion.

Caño, Annmarie. 2024. "Sabbaticals as Engines of Liberation." *Inside Higher Ed,* June 6, 2024. https://www.insidehighered.com/opinion/career-advice/advancing-faculty/2024/06/06/institutional-leaders-and-faculty-should-rethink.

Cano, Annmarie, Angelia M. Corley, Shannon M. Clark, and Sarah C. Martinez. 2018. "A Couple-Based Psychological Treatment for Chronic Pain and Relationship Distress." *Cognitive and Behavioral Practice* 25 (1): 119–134. https://doi.org/10.1016/j.cbpra.2017.02.003.

Castillo, Evan, and Lyss Welding. 2023. "Closed Colleges: List, Statistics, and Major Closures." BestColleges, last modified August 23, 2024. https://www.bestcolleges.com/research/closed-colleges-list-statistics-major-closures/.

Chavez-Dueñas, Nayeli Y., and Hector Y. Adames. 2020. "Intersectionality Awakening Model of Womanista: A Transnational Treatment Approach for Latinx Women." *Women and Therapy* 44 (1–2): 83–100. https://doi.org/10.1080/02703149.2020.1775022.

Chow, Rosalind. 2021. "Don't Just Mentor Women and People of Color. Sponsor Them." *Harvard Business Review*, June 30, 2021. https://hbr.org/2021/06/dont-just-mentor-women-and-people-of-color-sponsor-them.

Clance, Pauline R., and Suzanne A. Imes. 1978. "The Imposter Phenomenon in High Achieving Women: Dynamics and Therapeutic Intervention." *Psychotherapy: Theory, Research and Practice* 15 (3): 241–247.
https://doi.org/10.1037/h0086006.

Clark, Timothy R. 2020. *The Four Stages of Psychological Safety: Defining
the Path to Inclusion and Innovation*. Oakland, CA: Berrett-Koehler.

Coan, James A., and John M. Gottman. 2007. "The Specific Affect Coding
System (SPAFF)." In *Handbook of Emotion Elicitation and Assessment*,
edited by James Coan and John J. B. Allen, 267–285. Oxford: Oxford
University Press.

Comas-Díaz, Lillian. 2020. "Liberation Psychotherapy." In *Liberation
Psychology: Theory, Method, Practice, and Social Justice*, edited by Lillian
Comas-Díaz and Edil Torres Rivera, 169-185. Washington, DC:
American Psychological Association.

Comas-Díaz, Lillian. 2022. "Decolonization: A Personal Manifesto."
Women and Therapy 45 (4): 304–319. https://doi.org/10.1080
/02703149.2022.2125617.

Comas-Díaz, Lillian, and Edil Torres Rivera. 2020a. "Conclusion:
Liberation Psychology—Crossing Borders into New Frontiers." In
Liberation Psychology: Theory, Method, Practice, and Social Justice,
edited by Lillian Comas-Díaz and Edil Torres Rivera, 283–295.
Washington, DC: American Psychological Association.

Comas-Díaz, Lillian, and Edil Torres Rivera, eds. 2020b. *Liberation
Psychology: Theory, Method, Practice, and Social Justice*. Washington,
DC: American Psychological Association.

Cottom, Tressie M., Sally S. Hunnicutt, and Jennifer A. Johnson. 2018.
"The Ties That Corporatize: A Social Network Analysis of University
Presidents as Vectors of Higher Education Corporatization." SocArXiv,
May 22, 2018. https://doi.org/10.31235/osf.io/wpcfq.

Crenshaw, Kimberle. 1989. "Demarginalizing the Intersection of Race
and Sex: A Black Feminist Critique of Antidiscrimination Doctrine,
Feminist Theory and Antiracist Politics." *University of Chicago Legal
Forum* 1989 (1): article 8.

Crowley, Karlyn, and Jay Roberts. 2022. "Administrative Joy." *Inside
Higher Ed*, November 16, 2022. https://www.insidehighered.com
/advice/2022/11/17/how-administrators-can-find-more-joy-their
-work-and-life-opinion.

Curry, John R., Andrew L. Laws, and Jon C. Strauss. 2013. *Responsibility
Center Management: A Guide to Balancing Academic Entrepreneurship*

with Fiscal Responsibility. Washington, DC: National Association of College and University Business Officers.

DeSouza, Eros R. 2011. "Frequency Rates and Correlates of Contrapower Harassment in Higher Education." *Journal of Interpersonal Violence* 26 (1): 158–188. https://doi.org/10.1177/0886260510362878.

Dunbar-Ortiz, Roxanne. 2015. *An Indigenous Peoples' History of the United States: Four Hundred Years of Native American History from a Bottom-Up Perspective*. Boston: Beacon.

Dweck, Carol. 2006. *Mindset: The New Psychology of Success*. New York: Random House.

Edmondson, Amy C. 2018. *The Fearless Organization: Psychological Safety in the Workplace for Leaning, Innovation, and Growth*. Hoboken, NJ: Wiley.

Ekman, Paul, and Wallace V. Friesen. 1975. *Unmasking the Face: A Guide to Recognizing Emotions from Facial Clues*. Englewood Cliffs, NJ: Prentice-Hall.

Ellacuría, Ignacio. 1990. "Is a Different Kind of University Possible?" In *Towards a Society That Serves Its People*, edited by John Hassett and Hugh Lacey, 177–207. Washington, DC: Georgetown University Press.

Fernández, Jesica Siham. 2020. "Liberation Psychology of and for Transformative Justice: Centering *Acompañamiento* in Participatory Action Research." In *Liberation Psychology: Theory, Method, Practice, and Social Justice*, edited by Lillian Comas-Díaz and Edil Torres Rivera, 91–110. Washington, DC: American Psychological Association.

Fernández, Jesica Siham. 2022. "A *Mujerista* Liberation Psychology Perspective on *Testimonio* to Cultivate Decolonial Healing." *Women and Therapy* 45 (2–3): 131–156. https://dx.doi.org/10.1080/02703149.2022.2095101.

Flannery, Mary E. 2023. "The Mental Health Crisis on College Campuses." *National Education Association Today*, March 29, 2023. https://www.nea.org/nea-today/all-news-articles/mental-health-crisis-college-campuses.

Flores Niemann, Yolanda, Gabriella Gutiérrez y Muhs, and Carmen G. Gonzalez, eds. 2020. *Presumed Incompetent II: Race, Class, Power, and Resistance of Women in Academia*. Logan: Utah State University Press.

Freire, Paulo. (1970) 2000. *Pedagogy of the Oppressed*. New York: Seabury Books.

Freyd, Jennifer. 2018. "When Sexual Assault Victims Speak Out, Their Institutions Often Betray Them." *The Conversation*, January 11, 2018. http://theconversation.com/when-sexual-assault-victims-speak-out-their-institutions-often-betray-them-87050.

Freyd, Jennifer J. n.d. "What Is DARVO?" Accessed November 14, 2023. https://dynamic.uoregon.edu/jjf/defineDARVO.html.

Friedman, Edwin H. 2007. *A Failure of Nerve: Leadership in the Age of the Quick Fix*. New York: Seabury Books.

Gandolfo, Elizabeth O., and Laurel M. Potter. 2022. *Re-membering the Reign of God: The Decolonial Witness of El Salvador's Church of the Poor*. London: Lexington Books.

Gasman, Marybeth. 2022. *Doing the Right Thing: How Colleges and Universities Can Undo Systemic Racism in Faculty Hiring*. Princeton, NJ: Princeton University Press.

Gerbrandt, Nathan, Randy Grieser, and Vicki Enns. 2021. *A Little Book About Trauma-Informed Workplaces*. Winnipeg, MB: ACHIEVE.

Gómez, Jennifer M. 2023a. *The Cultural Betrayal of Black Women and Girls: A Black Feminist Approach to Healing from Sexual Abuse*. Washington, DC: American Psychological Association.

Gómez, Jennifer M. 2023b. "Is Academia a Dream-Killer?" *Inside Higher Ed*, August 25, 2023. https://www.insidehighered.com/opinion/career -advice/2023/08/25/moving-liberatory-thought-liberating-action -higher-ed-opinion.

González Stokas, Ariana. 2023. *Reparative Universities: Why Diversity Alone Won't Solve Racism in Higher Ed*. Baltimore: Johns Hopkins University Press.

Gretzinger, Erin, Maggie Hicks, Christa Dutton, and Jasper Smith. 2024. "Tracking Higher Ed's Dismantling of DEI." *Chronicle of Higher Education*, August 9, 2024. https://www.chronicle.com/article /tracking-higher-eds-dismantling-of-dei.

Gutiérrez, Gustavo. 1988. *A Theology of Liberation: History, Politics, and Salvation*. Maryknoll, NY: Orbis Books.

Gutiérrez y Muhs, Gabriella, Yolanda Flores Niemann, Carmen G. Gonzalez, and Angela P. Harris, eds. 2012. *Presumed Incompetent: The Intersections of Race and Class for Women in Academia*. Logan: Utah State University Press.

Hartling, Linda, and Elizabeth Sparks. 2008. "Relational-Cultural Practice: Working in a Nonrelational World." *Women and Therapy* 31 (2–4): 165–188. https://doi.org/10.1080/02703140802146332.

Hartling, Linda, and Elizabeth Sparks. 2010. "Relational-Cultural Practice: Working in a Nonrelational World." In *The Power of Connection: Recent Developments in Relational-Cultural Theory*, edited by Judith V. Jordan, 158–181. New York: Routledge.

Harvard Business Review. 2017. *HBR Guide to Emotional Intelligence*. Cambridge, MA: Harvard Business School Publishing.

Hass, Marjorie. 2021. *A Leadership Guide for Women in Higher Education*. Baltimore: Johns Hopkins University Press.

Hayes, Steven C., Jason B. Luoma, Frank W. Bond, Akihiko Masuda, and Jason Lillis. 2006. "Acceptance and Commitment Therapy: Model, Processes and Outcomes." *Behavior Research and Therapy* 44 (1): 1–25. https://doi.org/10.1016/j.brat.2005.06.006.

Hernandez, Jessica. 2022. *Fresh Banana Leaves: Healing Indigenous Landscapes Through Indigenous Science*. Berkeley, CA: North Atlantic Books.

Hersey, Tricia. 2022. *Rest Is Resistance: A Manifesto*. New York: Little, Brown Spark.

Higher Ed Dive. 2023. "A Look at Trends in College Consolidation Since 2016." Updated December 1, 2023. https://www.highereddive.com /news/how-many-colleges-and-universities-have-closed-since-2016 /539379/.

Ibarra, Herminia, and Rachel Simmons. 2023. "What Great Sponsors Do Differently." *Harvard Business Review*, January 19, 2023. https://hbr .org/2023/01/what-great-sponsors-do-differently.

Immerwahr, Daniel. 2019. *How to Hide an Empire: A History of the Greater United States*. New York: Farrar, Straus and Giroux.

Irwin, Veronique, Ke Wang, Tabitha Tezil, JJijun Zhang, Alison Filbey, Julie Jung, Farrah Bullock Mann, Rita Dilig, and Stephanie Parker. 2023. *Report on the Condition of Education 2023*. NCES 2023-144. Washington, DC: National Center for Education Statistics, US Department of Education. https://nces.ed.gov/pubsearch/pubsinfo .asp?pubid=2023144.

Isasi-Díaz, Ada María. 1996. *Mujerista Theology*. Maryknoll, NY: Orbis Books.

Jones, Kenneth, and Tema Okun. 2001. "White Supremacy Culture." In *Dismantling Racism: A Workbook for Social Change Groups*. ChangeWork, 2001. https://www.cwsworkshop.org/PARC_site_B/dr-culture.html.

Jordan, Judith V. 2010. *Relational-Cultural Therapy*. Washington, DC: American Psychological Association.

Kabat-Zinn, Jon. 1982. "An Outpatient Program in Behavioral Medicine for Chronic Pain Patients Based on the Practice of Mindfulness Meditation: Theoretical Considerations and Preliminary Results." *General Hospital Psychiatry* 4 (1): 33–47. https://dx.doi.org/10.1016 /0163-8343(82)90026-3.

Kabat-Zinn, Jon. 1990. *Full Catastrophe Living: Using the Wisdom of Your Body and Mind to Face Stress, Pain, and Illness*. New York: Bantam Books.

Keashly, Loraleigh. 2019. "Workplace Bullying, Mobbing and Harassment in Academe: Faculty Experience." In *Special Topics and Particular Occupations, Professions and Sectors. Handbooks of Workplace Bullying, Emotional Abuse and Harassment*, vol. 4, edited by Premilla D´Cruz, Ernesto Noronha, Loraleigh Keashly, and Stacy Tye-Williams. Singapore: Springer. https://doi.org/10.1007/978-981-10-5154-8_13-1.

Kelley, Robin D. G. 2016. "Black Study, Black Struggle." *Boston Review*, March 1, 2016. https://www.bostonreview.net/forum/robin-kelley -black-struggle-campus-protest/.

Kendi, Ibram X. 2017. *Stamped from the Beginning: The Definitive History of Racist Ideas in America*. New York: Bold Type Books.

Kimmerer, Robin Wall. 2015. *Braiding Sweetgrass: Indigenous Wisdom, Scientific Knowledge, and the Teachings of Plants*. Minneapolis, MN: Milkweed Editions.

Labaree, David F. 2017. *A Perfect Mess: The Unlikely Ascendancy of American Higher Education*. Chicago: University of Chicago Press.

Lassalle-Klein, Robert. 2014. *Blood and Ink: Ignacio Ellacuría, Jon Sobrino, and the Jesuit Martyrs of the University of Central America*. Maryknoll, NY: Orbis Books.

Lederman, Doug. 2023. "Majority of Americans Lack Confidence in Value of 4-Year Degree." *Inside Higher Ed*, April 3, 2023. https://www .insidehighered.com/news/2023/04/03/majority-americans-lack -confidence-value-four-year-degree.

LeMura, Linda. 2021. "Webinar for the AJCU Leadership Institute." Lecture, Association of Jesuit Colleges and Universities, Syracuse, NY, March 2, 2021.

Malhotra, Ruchika T. 2022. *Inclusion on Purpose: An Intersectional Approach to Creating a Culture of Belonging at Work*. Cambridge, MA: MIT Press.

Martín-Baró, Ignacio. 1994. *Writings for a Liberation Psychology*. Translated by Adrianne Aron and Shawn Corne. Cambridge, MA: Harvard University Press.

Maslach, Christina, Wilmar B. Schaufeli, and Michael P. Leiter. 2001. "Job Burnout." *Annual Review of Psychology* 52 (1): 397–422. https://doi .org/10.1146/annurev.psych.52.1.397.

Mathews, Tayler J. 2017. "Institutional Cultural Betrayal: The Loss of HBCU Pride." Medium, October 29, 2017. https://medium.com

/@FeministSnob/institutional-cultural-betrayal-the-loss-of-hbcu-pride
-d329d2075141.

Matthew, Patricia A., ed. 2016. *Written/Unwritten: Diversity and the Hidden Truths of Tenure*. Durham: University of North Carolina Press.

Mayuzumi, Kimine. 2017. "Developing Your Own Academic 'Index': An Interview with Dr. Beronda Montgomery." *Being Lazy and Slowing Down* (blog), November 28, 2017. https://lazyslowdown.com /developing-your-own-academic-index/.

Melidona, Danielle, Benjamin G. Cecil, Alexander Cassell, and Hollie M. Chessman. 2023. *The American College President: 2023 Edition— Executive Summary*. Washington, DC: American Council on Education.

Montero, Maritza. 2016. "Psychology of Liberation Revised (a Critique of Critique)." In *The Palgrave Handbook of Critical Social Psychology*, edited by Brendan Gough, 147–161. London: Palgrave Macmillan.

Montgomery, Beronda L. 2020a. "Academic Leadership: Gatekeeping or Groundskeeping?" *Journal of Values-Based Leadership* 13 (2): article 16. https://doi.org/10.22543/0733.132.1316.

Montgomery, Beronda L. 2020b. "The Radical Thing I Did in Higher Education." Beronda L. Montgomery's blog, June 12, 2020. https:// www.berondamontgomery.com/category/affirmation/.

Montgomery, Beronda L. 2021. *Lessons from Plants*. Cambridge, MA: Harvard University Press.

Moody, JoAnn. 2011. *Faculty Diversity: Removing the Barriers*. 2nd ed. New York: Routledge.

Mrig, Amit, and Patrick Sanaghan. 2017. *The Skills Future Higher-Ed Leaders Need to Succeed*. Denver: Academic Impressions.

Muth, John J. 2002. *The Three Questions: Based on a Story by Leo Tolstoy*. New York: Scholastic.

Neville, Helen A., Nidia Ruedas-Gracia, B. Andi Lee, Nimot Ogunfemi, Amir H. Maghsoodi, Della V. Mosley, Teresa D. LaFrombroise, and Michelle Fine. 2021. "The Public Psychology for Liberation Training Model: A Call to Transform the Discipline." *American Psychologist* 76 (8): 1248–1265. https://doi.org/10.1037/amp0000887.

Okun, Tema. 2023. "Introduction to the Website." White Supremacy Culture, last modified August 2023. https://www.whitesupremacy culture.info/about.html.

Oluo, Ijeoma. 2018. *So You Want to Talk About Race*. New York: Seal.

O'Meara, KerryAnn, Alexandra Kuvaeva, Gudrun Nyunt, Chelsea Wauga- man, and Rose Jackson. 2017. "Asked More Often: Gender Differences in Faculty Workload in Research Universities and the Work Interactions

That Shape Them." *American Educational Research Journal* 54 (6): 1154–1186. https://doi.org/10.3102/0002831217716767.

Opie, Tina, and Beth A. Livingston. 2022. *Shared Sisterhood: How to Take Collective Action for Racial and Gender Equity at Work.* Cambridge, MA: Harvard Business Review Press.

Painter, Nell I. 2011. *The History of White People.* New York: W. W. Norton.

Pope-Ruark, Rebecca. 2022. *Unraveling Faculty Burnout: Pathways to Reckoning and Renewal.* Baltimore: Johns Hopkins University Press.

Quiñones-Rosado, Raúl. 2020. "Liberation Psychology and Racism." In *Liberation Psychology: Theory, Method, Practice, and Social Justice,* edited by Lillian Comas-Díaz and Edil Torres Rivera, 53–68. Washington, DC: American Psychological Association.

Rahim-Dillard, Salwa. 2021. "How Inclusive Is Your Leadership?" *Harvard Business Review,* April 19, 2021. https://hbr.org/2021/04/how-inclusive-is-your-leadership.

Ray, Victor. 2019. "A Theory of Racialized Organizations." *American Sociological Review* 84 (1): 26–53. https://doi.org/10.1177/0003122418822335.

Rennison, Callie, and Bonomi, Amy, eds. 2020. *Women Leading Change in Academia: Breaking the Glass Ceiling, Cliff, and Slipper.* Solana Beach, CA: Cognella.

Rogelberg, Steven G. 2019. *The Surprising Science of Meetings: How You Can Lead Your Team to Peak Performance.* Oxford: Oxford University Press.

Rogers, Carl R. 1946. "Significant Aspects of Client-Centered Therapy." *American Psychologist* 1 (10): 415–422. https://doi.org/10.1037/h0060866.

Rowland, Deborah. 2017. *Still Moving: How to Lead Mindful Change.* Chichester, UK: John Wiley and Sons.

Ruvio, Ayalla, and Forrest V. Morgeson. 2022. "Are You Being Quiet Fired?" *Harvard Business Review,* November 7, 2022. https://hbr.org/2022/11/are-you-being-quiet-fired.

Saad, Layla. 2020. *Me and White Supremacy: Combat Racism, Change the World, and Become a Good Ancestor.* Naperville, IL: Sourcebooks.

Scott, Kim. 2021. *Just Work: How to Root Out Bias, Prejudice, and Bullying to Build a Kick-Ass Culture of Inclusivity.* New York: St. Martin's.

Settles, Isis H., NiCole T. Buchanan, and Kristie Dotson. 2019. "Scrutinized but Not Recognized: (In)visibility and Hypervisibility Experiences of Faculty of Color." *Journal of Vocational Behavior* 113:62–74. https://doi.org/10.1016/j.jvb.2018.06.003.

Settles, Isis H., Martinique K. Jones, NiCole T. Buchanan, and Kristie Dotson. 2021. "Epistemic Exclusion: Scholar(ly) Devaluation That Marginalizes Faculty of Color." *Journal of Diversity in Higher Education* 14 (4): 493–507. https://doi.org/10.1037/dhe0000174.

Silf, Margaret. 2007. *Wise Choices: A Spiritual Guide to Making Life's Decisions.* New York: BlueBridge.

Smith Carly P., and Jennifer J. Freyd. 2013. "Dangerous Safe Havens: Institutional Betrayal Exacerbates Sexual Trauma." *Journal of Traumatic Stress* 26: 119-124. http://doi.wiley.com/10.1002/jts.21778.

Smith, Carly P., and Jennifer J. Freyd. 2014. "Institutional Betrayal." *American Psychologist* 69 (6): 575–587. https://doi.org/10.1037/a0037564.

Social Sciences Feminist Network Research Interest Group. 2017. "The Burden of Invisible Work in Academia Social Inequalities and Time Use in Five University Departments." *Humboldt Journal of Social Relations* 39:228–245. https://www.jstor.org/stable/90007882.

Stein, Sharon. 2022. *Unsettling the University: Confronting the Colonial Foundations of US Higher Education.* Baltimore: Johns Hopkins University Press.

Stewart, Abigail, and Virginia Valian. 2018. *An Inclusive Academy: Achieving Diversity and Excellence.* Cambridge, MA: MIT Press.

Swartout, Kevin M., Jess Neumann-Kersten, M. Dickstein, and M. Aguilar. 2023. *State of the CDO Survey Report.* Rankin Climate.

Tallbear, Kim. 2019. "Caretaking Relations, Not American Dreaming." *Kalfou* 6 (1). https://doi.org/10.15367/kf.v6i1.228.

Thomas, Kecia M., ed. 2020. *Diversity Resistance in Organizations.* 2nd ed. Abingdon, UK: Routledge.

Thomas, Kecia M., Juanita Johnson-Bailey, Rosemary E. Phelps, Ny M. Tran, and Lindsay Johnson. 2013. "Women of Color at Midcareer: Going from Pet to Threat." In *The Psychological Health of Women of Color: Intersections, Challenges, and Opportunities,* edited by Lillian Comas-Diáz and Beverly Greene, 275–286. Santa Barbara, CA: Praeger.

Tulshyan, Ruchika, and Jodi-Ann Burney. 2021. "Stop Telling Women They Have Imposter Syndrome." *Harvard Business Review,* February 11, 2021. https://hbr.org/2021/02/stop-telling-women-they-have-imposter-syndrome.

Watkins, Michael D. 2014. *The First 90 Days: Proven Strategies for Getting Up to Speed Faster and Smarter.* Updated and expanded ed. Cambridge, MA: Harvard Business Review Press.

Weissman, Sara. 2022. "Students Who 'Stand to Lose the Most.'" *Inside Higher Ed*, October 20, 2022. https://www.insidehighered.com/news/2022/10/21/high-food-and-housing-insecurity-community-colleges.

Williams, Damon A., Joseph B. Berger, and Shederick A. McClendon. 2005. *Toward a Model of Inclusive Excellence and Change in Postsecondary Institutions*. Washington, DC: Association for American Colleges and Universities.

Williams, Joan. 2001. *Unbending Gender: Why Family and Work Conflict and What to Do About It*. Oxford: Oxford University Press.

INDEX